PASSION FOR THE EARTH

The Orbis Series *Ecology and Justice* includes books that seek to integrate an understanding of the Earth as an interconnected life system with concerns for just and sustainable social systems that benefit the entire Earth.

Viewing the present moment as a time for responsible creativity, the Series seeks authors who speak to ecojustice concerns and who bring into dialogue perspectives from the Christian community, from the world's religions, from secular and scientific circles, and from new paradigms of thought and action.

Also in the series

ECOLOGY AND JUSTICE SERIES

PASSION FOR THE EARTH

Sean McDonagh

SSND JPIC

ORBIS BOOKS

Maryknoll, New York 10545

The Catholic Foreign Mission Society of America (Maryknoll) recruits and trains people for overseas missionary service. Through Orbis Books, Maryknoll aims to foster the international dialogue that is essential to mission. The books published, however, reflect the opinions of their authors and are not meant to represent the official position of the society.

© Sean McDonagh SSC 1994

Published in the United States by Orbis Books
Maryknoll, New York 10545–0308

First published in the UK by Geoffrey Chapman, a Cassell imprint, London

Printed and bound in Great Britain

ORBIS/ISBN 1–57075–021–1

Cataloging-in-Publication Data for this book is available from the Library of Congress, Washington, D.C.

Contents

I would like to thank the many Columbans, priests, sisters and lay people, who shared their passion for peace, justice and the integrity of creation with me during the past few years. The fingerprints of Vincent Busch and Christina Herman are clearly visible in the text. Annette Honan alerted me to some important oversights in an earlier draft. The staff of Greenpeace, Ireland, especially Clare O'Grady-Walshe, made available a wealth of information on many contemporary ecological issues. Ruth McCurry and Fiona McKenzie of Geoffrey Chapman and the copy-editor, Anne Mathew, provided much-needed professional advice and helped me meet the publication deadline.

A special word of thanks to Marie Boyle, my colleague here at the Justice and Peace office in St Columban's, Dalgan Park, Navan, Co. Meath. She has guided this book through every stage of its genesis from the original idea to the final proof-reading. Her meticulous attention to detail and thorough grasp of the issues has improved this book immeasurably. I, needless to say, take responsibility for any shortcomings. At a personal level I am grateful to my mother, Eileen, my sister, Maire, and my many friends for their constant support while I was writing this book.

Abbreviations

BCSD	Business Council for Sustainable Development
CAFOD	Catholic Fund for Overseas Development
CEGB	Central Electricity Generating Board
CNN	Cable News Network
CPPs	Country Programme Papers
DSU	Dispute Settlement Understanding
EGAT	Electric Generating Authority in Thailand
EPA	Environmental Protection Agency
EU	European Union
FAO	Food and Agriculture Organization
GAST	General Agreement on Sustainable Trade
GATS	General Agreement on Trade in Services
GATT	General Agreement on Tariffs and Trade
GDP	Gross Domestic Product
GEF	Global Environment Facility (at World Bank)
GNP	Gross National Product
IAEA	International Atomic Energy Agency
IBRD	International Bank for Reconstruction and Development
IDA	International Development Agency
IFC	International Finance Corporation
ILO	International Labour Organization
IMF	International Monetary Fund
IPCC	Intergovernmental Panel on Climate Change
IPRs	Intellectual Property Rights
ITU	International Telecommunications Union
JPIC	Justice, Peace and the Integrity of Creation

MFA	Multi-Fibre Arrangement
NAFTA	North American Free Trade Agreement
NASA	National Aeronautics and Space Administration
NGO	Non-government Organization
NICs	Newly Industrialized Countries
OAU	Organization of African Unity
OECD	Organization of Economic Co-operation and Development
OED	Operations Evaluation Department
PFPs	Policy Framework Papers
PICs	Products of Incomplete Combustion
SAL	Structural Adjustment Loan
SAPs	Structural Adjustment Programmes
SRC	Sollicitudo Rei Socialis
TNCs	Transnational Corporations
TRIPs	Trade-related Intellectual Property Rights
UNCED	United Nations Conference on Environment and Development
UNCTAD	United Nations Commission on Trade and Development
UNDP	United Nations Development Programme
UNICEF	United Nations International Children's Emergency Fund
WCC	World Council of Churches
WHO	World Health Organization
WTO	World Trade Organization

In memory of my father, who loved his garden

Introduction

THE GLOBAL ECONOMY, which is characteristic of our world today, means that the countries of the North and South are interdependent. Similarly, developmental and environmental issues are inextricably linked. Unfortunately, this state of affairs has not led to widespread prosperity, justice, or environmental sustainability or renewal. In fact, the obsession with economic growth which is a feature of the global economy is impoverishing the majority of peoples of the world and endangering the planet.

The following parable captures some aspects of this development and ecological crisis. It highlights the inability of many people, especially those in leadership roles in institutions, to deal with the widening gap between rich and poor and the rampant destruction of the environment in an effective and systematic way.[1]

* * *

A group of people were invited to attend a banquet in a beautiful medieval castle situated in a magnificent courtyard. It was a splendid feast with a profusion of sumptuous dishes, a delicious range of wines and other drinks, superb service and an excellent orchestra to entertain the guests as they ate. The food was so sumptuous and the drink so delicious that the guests simply couldn't get enough. They continued to gorge themselves long after the point of satiation.

As the night wore on, instead of ending the meal, relaxing and going home, the revellers became more and more intent on securing additional helpings of the mouth-watering food. Their demands became so voracious that all the food was consumed. The master of the house, in order to avoid embarrassment, sent out his servants, backed by the militia, to collect more food from the poor inhabitants in the surrounding countryside.

Fuel to cook the food also ran out. The cooks ordered some servants to begin chopping away at the timber pillars that supported the roof in order to get firewood to continue cooking. After a while some pillars began to sag a little and cracks appeared in the ceiling. But the servants and the banqueters were so absorbed in the meal that they were completely unaware of the long-term implications of what they were doing. They had no time to consider that, unless they stopped hacking at the supporting pillars, the ceiling would eventually come crashing down on their heads. Needless to say they did not give a thought for the hundreds of servants living in the castle compound who would also perish if the castle collapsed.

The din, buzz and activity in the kitchen and dining hall were electrifying. People were milling around the cooking stoves, shouting orders for more food and eating with relish. Yet not everyone was caught up in the frenzy. A small number of people stood by the doors with neither plates nor glasses in their hands. Some, with what might be called a social justice perspective, denounced the diners, pointed out that the heavy cost of the meal was being borne by the poor in the surrounding countryside. Others, with an eye for the environmental consequences, aware that the beams were already sagging and that a tragedy was imminent, implored the diners to end the meal and thus avert the disaster.

A few of those eating would occasionally stop to listen to their heartfelt pleas; they might even cast a fleeting glance towards the ceiling. But as soon as a waiter with food came close they would lose interest and join in the scramble for more. The majority of those who were celebrating, however, didn't take any notice at all. They were simply so engrossed in the meal that nothing else really mattered.

* * *

This book is an attempt to elucidate some of the issues involved in this parable and to look at how they are being addressed by the churches, especially the leadership of the Catholic Church. While my presentation will draw on many experts in the fields of development and the environment, I am writing from the perspective of a missionary.

Between 1969 and 1989 I lived in the Philippines. During that time I witnessed two trends, both at the national and international level. The first was the impact that our modern, technological, industrial and consumer society was having on the earth, with the destruction of rainforests, soils and marine ecosystems. The second was the increasing gap between rich and poor nations, as well as between rich and poor in individual countries. Since 1989 I have been central co-ordinator for Justice, Peace and the Integrity of Creation (JPIC) for the worldwide Columban Missionary Society. During my visits to countries in Asia and Latin America I have seen similar trends or heard about them from my fellow missionaries.

The demands which are made by our modern, affluent way of living are impoverishing the poor. Multinational companies, international finance agencies and voracious nations are exploiting the poor – demanding ever-cheaper labour and a constant supply of cheap natural resources. Poorer nations are forced to sell their valuable resources in order to service crippling interest on debts set by richer nations and institutions. In addition, they are seduced into following the wasteful lifestyles of their exploiters, which only compounds their already worsening plight. The results are that the poor become poorer, hungrier, more vulnerable and more disenfranchised.

This same system is also killing the earth itself. Numerous books (including my own: *To Care for the Earth* and *The Greening of the Church*) and television documentaries in recent years have shown the rampant damage to particular regions and the planet as a whole. In this book I will focus on the fact that modern economic patterns of production, distribution, consumption, trade and development are taxing and even breaching the regenerative capacity of the biosphere. This is a very serious indictment as it entails diminishing life on earth for all future generations of humans and other creatures.

The constant teaching of the Hebrew and Christian scriptures and all the Christian churches is that the goods of this world are meant to sustain all human life on earth. The devastation of the earth by such modern means is condemned by the Gospel of Jesus. The thrust of that Gospel can be summed up, without distortion, in the text of John 10:10 – 'I have come that they may have life, and have it to the full.' Anything that diminishes life sins against this.

The latter part of the book will explore how the cry of the poor and the cry of the earth challenge dominant institutions in our society, especially the Catholic Church. Few institutions have coped creatively or adequately with the impact of our worldwide industrial society on the Two-Thirds World or the earth. Yet if abundant life for all is to be attained then every institution, including religious institutions, must begin to bring ideas about justice, peace and the integrity of creation into the very core of its message as a matter of urgency.

Through this book I hope to arouse and focus concern among Christians so that we can respond to this challenge of the contemporary world in a creative and comprehensive way. I am convinced that moral and religious values can provide individuals and communities with the psychic energy to challenge our present earth-consuming way of life. A truly appropriate religious vision can provide the springboard for that imaginative leap which will be necessary to enable people to design new, more sustainable cultures. In this way of living the emphasis will need to be more on sharing rather than consumption, long-term needs rather than immediate gratification, and community values and ecosystem needs rather than individual profit or aggrandizement. In other words, it will encourage people to share the earth more equitably and to live on it in a lighter, less destructive way.

DEFINING THE WORLD

A word about the terminology which is commonly used in development debate may not be out of place. Until recently, for those involved in development work, the world was divided into three groupings – First, Second and Third. The First World referred to the industrialized countries of Europe, the United States and Canada, Japan, Australia and New Zealand. A few countries like South Korea, Taiwan, Singapore and Hong Kong have joined this club within the past decade. Even though Australia and New Zealand are located in the southern hemisphere, and some of the newly industrialized countries are in the tropics, the majority of industrialized countries are in the northern hemisphere and this bloc is often referred to today as the North. To add to the confusion,.

the élite in the South are often referred to as a North in the South, while the new poor in the North are called the South in the North. The Second World consisted of the socialist countries of eastern Europe, the USSR, China, North Korea and Cuba. With the demise of Marxism, the Second World could now be considered to be on the list of endangered species! Only North Korea, Cuba and to a lesser extent the People's Republic of China survive as Marxist, centrally planned economies.

The Third World, often also referred to as 'underdeveloped', included the countries of Africa, Latin America and much of Asia. This bloc, in more recent times, has been referred to as the South. The term 'Third World' was coined in the 1950s in France. It was meant to denote the economic, social and political dependency which still bound the newly independent countries to their former colonial masters or other Western economies. The value of the term is that it stresses the systemic and causal relationship between the rich and poor countries. It alerts people to the fact that economic decisions taken in Washington, Tokyo or London have a direct impact on the lives of people thousands of miles away. While 'Third World' is less offensive and more accurate than 'underdeveloped', it still has major disadvantages. In a hierarchical world it is, after all, third and last. This is why many people now prefer the term Two-Thirds World. This term, at least, has the advantage of being more demographically accurate, since two-thirds of the population of the world live there.

I will use the term Third World sparingly in this book. There are some situations, however, in which it is almost impossible to avoid using it, for example when referring to Third World debt.

Finally, all dollar amounts quoted throughout will be US dollars, unless noted otherwise.

NOTE
1 I wrote this parable after reading a sentence by Fazlun M. Khalid in the Preface to *Islam and Ecology* (London: Cassell, 1992), p. ix.

CHAPTER 1

Impoverishing
the poor

MOST PEOPLE WILL ADMIT that our modern, industrial, throw-away society has benefited a number of individuals and groups. It has brought huge profits and a growing control of world production and markets to multinational corporations and financial institutions. It has brought innumerable comforts and incredible possibilities for consumer choice to the rich and middle classes in Northern countries and the élite in the Two-Thirds World. All these groups add up to about 1 billion people, which is less than one in five of all people living today. The down side of this international economy is that four-fifths of the world's population has not been served by it, and a significant percentage, especially those living in the South, have been impoverished by its operations.

One simple way of judging the success of any economic system is to look at how it provides for the basic needs of people. Every person, most would agree, needs an adequate intake of nutritious food, adequate clothing, a decent place to live and access to basic education and health care. The present economic system fails to deliver most of the above to even a fraction of the world's population. And the situation is deteriorating. In the early 1980s, the World Bank and the UN Food and Agriculture Organization (FAO) estimated that between 700 million and 1 billion people lived in absolute poverty. Robert McNamara, a former President of.

the World Bank, described absolute poverty as a condition of life so limited by malnutrition, illiteracy, disease, squalid surroundings, high infant mortality, and low life expectancy as to be beneath any reasonable definition of human dignity.

McNamara was concerned about the world situation in the late 1970s. In 1994 most indicators suggest that poverty has increased dramatically in sub-Saharan Africa, and to a lesser extent in most of Latin America and significant areas of South and South-East Asia. The number living in absolute poverty in 1992 stood at 1.2 billion. This included 560 million rural women and millions of children with mothers as the sole parent.[1] What is more alarming is that while the percentage of the world's population who are in this category dropped steadily between the 1950s and the 1970s, it began to climb again during the 1980s, when the world's population living in extreme poverty increased from 22.3 per cent to 23.4 per cent. This increase took place despite three decades of development, bilateral aid and the activities of the multilateral lending agencies, which declare they are committed to reducing world poverty.

THE RICH GET RICHER

Modern development theory and practice assumes that economic improvement will take place if the volume of economic activity is increased. There is an acceptance of the fact that during the initial stages of 'development' there will probably be a concentration of wealth in the hands of the rich. However, it is claimed that when the benefits of capital accumulation and growth have reached a certain threshold, significant economic benefits will 'trickle down' and enhance the lives of the poor.

Unfortunately, this is not the way things operate in the real world where politics, economics and ecology meet. What happens, in fact, is that the gap between the rich and the poor, on a national and worldwide stage, increases as income distribution becomes more lopsided. In the period between 1965 and 1984 the Gross National Product (GNP) in many countries increased. The per capita income for wealthy nations in North America, Europe and Japan almost tripled. This growth spurt is often held up as an example of how well the system is working. A closer look at the figures tells a different story. The annual per capita increase in the North – $270 – far outstripped the $7 increase in poorer countries. Furthermore, it is most likely that the $7 increase did not go to the most needy. Income distribution is often very skewed in the Two-Thirds World.

On average, the richest 10 per cent, for example, have more than 33 per cent of the income, while the poorest 40 per cent receive only 15 per cent.

Every now and then a report, a statistic or a particularly graphic photo captures the immense difference between the living standards of the rich and the poor. The *Guardian* (10 December 1993) achieved this with a simple question: What's the difference between Tanzania and Goldman Sachs? One is an African country that makes $2.2 billion per annum and shares it among 25 million people; the other is an investment bank that made $2.6 billion profit in 1992 and shares that among 161 people.

It is important to emphasize that this yawning gap has not always existed. According to the Swiss economist Paul Bairoch the per capita Gross National Product for 'developed' and 'underdeveloped' countries in 1750 was more or less similar. In 1930 it had grown to a ratio of four to one and by 1990 eight to one. The tragedy of recent decades is that, despite the fine rhetoric about poverty reduction, the gap is growing at an alarming rate. According to *Human Development Report*, published by the United Nations Development Programme (UNDP) in 1992:

In 1960, the richest 20 per cent of the world's population had incomes 30 times greater than the poorest 20 per cent. By 1990, the richest 20 per cent were getting 60 times more. And this comparison is based on the distribution between rich and poor countries. Adding to the maldistribution within countries, the richest 20 per cent of the world's people get at least 150 times more than the poorest 20 per cent.

During the 1980s the neo-liberal economic policies championed by Margaret Thatcher in Britain and Ronald Reagan in the USA were thrust upon the Third World by both the World Bank and the International Monetary Fund (IMF). As a result the share of global wealth enjoyed by the Third World fell from 22 per cent to 18 per cent.[2] As of 1990 the top 20 per cent Northern minority enjoyed 82.7 per cent of the world's Gross National Product, 81.9 per cent of world trade, 94.6 per cent of all commercial lending, 80.6 per cent of all domestic savings, and 94 per cent of all research and development.[3]

The rich, especially those managing corporations, have also enjoyed remarkable tax breaks in recent years. In their book *America: Who Really Pays the Taxes?*, Pulitzer prize-winning reporters Donal L. Barlett and James B. Steele show that the rich avail themselves of a maze of tax loopholes and the expertise of an army of accountants and lawyers to avoid paying their share of taxes. For example, the authors point out that in 1989, 1,081 people with an income above $200,000 ended up paying no federal tax at all.

The rich also own much of the media and can mount very successful PR campaigns to promote their interests. One of their complaints in recent years is that corporate taxes have risen intolerably. In reality the opposite has happened. Since the 1950s taxes for corporations and the very rich have fallen by about one-third. During the same period the tax burden borne by the middle class has risen by a massive 329 per cent.[4] Such historical data do little to stop the rich from complaining about burdensome taxes. Peter Morgan, the Director-General of the Institute of Directors in Britain, commenting on the potential negative impact of the recent GATT agreement, stated that 'Our markets will be open to imports produced by highly competitive firms in economies which are not bogged down under the weight of excessive regulations and taxation'.[5]

In the 1980s many Republican politicians in the US and Conservatives in Britain also criticized the social welfare system as being too large, too expensive and an incentive to idleness. They were ably abetted by sections of the media who contributed to the anti-welfare mood by regularly running stories on dole scroungers.

Once again the facts are quite different. There are many recipients of government financial support but they are not all poor people living on welfare cheques. In the US, for example, three times as much housing subsidy has gone to the top fifth of the population as to the bottom 20 per cent.[6] Much of the prosperity of Silicon Valley in California is directly dependent on the Defense Department's subsidy to the armaments industry. And by bailing out the Savings and Loans institutions the US government unintentionally subsidizes golf courses, resorts, office buildings and expensive housing stock to the tune of several hundred billion dollars.[7] While public money is allocated for a variety of purposes, in the final analysis the rich do much better than the poor who need it most.

THE IMPACT ON THE POOR

In individual Southern countries, including ones that have great natural wealth like Brazil, the effect of neo-liberal economic policies on the lives of the poor is disastrous. In 1986 Cardinal Arns, the Archbishop of São Paulo, presented a submission to the North–South Commission. In it he gave details of how impoverishment can increase even in a country like Brazil, which had growth rates of over 7 per cent during the late 1960s and 1970s. According to the Archbishop, in the period between 1961 and 1964, 27 million Brazilians or 38 per cent of the population were underfed. By 1984, after over a decade of the so-called economic miracle, 86 million people or 65 per cent of the population were underfed. The export-oriented economic policies had a devastating impact on food production. They promoted hunger and malnutrition because land which formerly grew food was now devoted to cash crops for export. Between 1977 and 1984 the per capita production of staple foods like rice, black beans, manioc and potatoes fell by 13 per cent. During the same period the per capita output of agriculture products for export – soya beans, oranges, cotton, peanuts and tobacco – jumped by 15 per cent. In the case of soya beans, production jumped from 1 million tons in 1970 to 18.5 million in 1985.

Whilst the poverty which exists in Northern countries cannot be compared with the deprivation of the urban slums in the Third World, nevertheless it does destroy the lives of many people and alienates them from the wider community. This disparity has grown in industrialized countries in recent years. Early in 1990 Kevin Phillips, in *The Politics of Rich and Poor*, showed that during the Reagan administration there was an unprecedented redistribution of income in favour of the rich. The share of national income enjoyed by the top 1 per cent grew from 7 per cent in 1977 to 11 per cent in 1988. That top 1 per cent had received a 60 per cent income gain during the previous decade.[8] As a result the number of millionaires jumped by 300 per cent between 1980 and 1988. But the percentage of people living in poverty also grew. US Census figures published in September 1992 show that the number of people with incomes below the poverty level increased by 2.1 million to 35.7 million in 1991. The percentage living in poverty stood at 14.2 per cent in 1991.[9]

The same pattern of discrepancy between the rich and the poor exists in Europe. The *Guardian* (1 July 1993) reported that statistics gathered by the Department of Social Security in Britain show that the poorest families' income fell 14 per cent during the Thatcher years. As usual, women and children are most affected by the increase in poverty. A comprehensive survey of London's primary schools found that in 1993 one in four pupils were entitled to free school meals as against one in six in 1991. In some of the poorer boroughs more than half the pupils are now receiving free lunches.

Nationwide the gap between the rich and the poor in Britain has increased since 1979. Andrew Glyn and David Millband, writing in the *Guardian* (25 April 1994), stated that the top 1 per cent of income earners received 93 times as much per head in tax cuts between 1979 and 1992 as the bottom 50 per cent. As a result of monetarist economic policies under recent Conservative governments the gap between the highest and the lowest paid has increased to levels last seen in 1886.[10]

Even Germany, for decades the envy of almost every other European country, is not exempt from the poverty trap for significant numbers of its people. A nationwide survey on poverty published in early 1994 claimed that 7 million people live in poverty. A greater proportion of the poor live in the former East Germany. Yet the report maintained that there is a growing division between the poor and the rich in both parts of Germany.[11]

The bulk of the new poor in Northern countries are the unemployed. The figures for mass unemployment have risen steadily over the past decade. In 1993, for example, over 17 million people were unemployed in the European Union (EU) and the figure is likely to grow substantially. While politicians talk at national and international fora about policies to promote job creation many analysts are sceptical.

The present global economic policies do not promote job creation. It makes more sense economically to invest heavily in new, more sophisticated technologies which replace people with machines. It is also clear that expectations that the new technologies will create new employment niches, as happened during the early phases of the Industrial Revolution, are unrealistic. Structural unemployment and consequent growing impoverishment will be with us for the foreseeable future unless fundamental issues are addressed.[12]

THIRD WORLD DEBT

One of the main mechanisms for impoverishing the South, in recent years, is the Third World debt (which amounted to $1,700 billion in March 1994), where large amounts of money from poor countries are transferred to rich countries. The debts were contracted in the 1970s when Northern banks were flush with petrodollars and wished to recycle them, in the process making a hefty profit. Northern governments also knew that the loans were being made to repressive regimes, like the Marcos regime in the Philippines. (It is common knowledge that this regime embezzled billions of dollars and squandered the rest on projects which were of little benefit to the majority of poor people in the country.) In the early 1980s the debts ballooned out of control. Some of the blame for the disaster, undoubtedly, must be laid at the door of Southern politicians and their economic advisers. But it is important to highlight the external factors which exacerbated the problems, over which Third World leaders had no control. These included currency fluctuations, often brought about by Structural Adjustment Programmes (SAPs); the rise in interest rates internationally, caused by pressures within the US economy; and the dramatic drop in commodity prices which accompanied the recession in industrialized countries.

Servicing these debts is an enormous burden for most Southern countries today. Between 1982 and 1990 Jamaica spent $4.2 billion servicing its foreign debt. Even so the debt increased by 55 per cent. Susan George in *The Debt Boomerang* gives some mind-boggling data on the figures involved in this transfer of wealth to the rich.[13] During the period 1982 to 1990 there was a net transfer of $418 billion from the poor South to the rich North. To give some idea of the huge sums involved she calculates that the poor of the world have financed the modern equivalent of six Marshall Plans for the rich through debt servicing alone. (The Marshall Plan involved the United States making aid available to European countries in the wake of World War II to rebuild their shattered economies.)

Right through the debt crisis in the 1980s the World Bank and the International Monetary Fund (IMF) acted as policeman for the Northern capitalist system. They imposed Structural Adjustment Programmes (SAPs) on Third World countries which were experiencing severe debt problems as a condition for receiving further loans. SAPs are based on narrow monetarist economic policies. They are designed to improve a country's balance of payments and foreign investment climate by reducing government spending and promoting export-oriented enterprises. Though there are slight variations from country to country, the common menu contained in the SAPs package includes currency devaluation, trade liberalization, business deregulation, privatization of government-owned commercial operations, cuts in public spending – usually health and education – tight credit policies, a wage freeze, and higher interest rates.

The policies of the World Bank and IMF have been ineffective in reducing poverty and promoting sustainability, however. The reason is simple: they failed to address the real causes of growing poverty and environmental degradation in Third World countries. SAPs have aggravated rather than cured the problems of many Third World countries. They have as much chance of effecting a cure as blood-letting did in previous centuries: rather than cure the sickness, it further weakened the patient. In the 1980s, SAPs caused starvation, illiteracy and political and social breakdown. In the natural world they resulted in extensive and irreversible destruction to important ecosystems like the rainforests and marine environments. The human suffering entailed in this was summed up in a 1990 UNICEF report: 'Hundreds of thousands of the developing world's children have given their lives to pay their countries' debts, and many millions more are still paying the interest with their malnourished minds and bodies.'[14]

Despite all the attempts at debt relief – which include the Baker Plan, the Brady Plan and the Trinidad Terms, to mention only three – and the huge sums that have already been repaid, the size of the Third World debt continues to grow. While a number of commercial banks and some countries have agreed to some debt reduction and rescheduling the World Bank and the IMF have refused to reduce or reschedule the debt owed to them. These debts now stand at $278 billion or 17 per cent of the total debt. One way or another it is clear that the Third World debt will continue to increase unless drastic action is taken.

The Third World debt (to which I will return in Chapter 4) illustrates how unjust the present economic system is. It does not serve the needs of the peoples of the world in an equitable way. It has led to the 'overdevelopment' of a few countries and the 'underdevelopment' of most of the rest. If our world is meant to support all life on earth, and all humans in a way that allows them to live in dignity, then the present economic and political system which promotes such inequalities is clearly failing.

NOTES

1 *The State of World Rural Poverty: An Inquiry into Its Causes and Consequences* (Rome: The International Fund for Agricultural Development, 1992).
2 Tim Lang and Colin Hines, *The New Protectionism: Protecting the Future Against Free Trade* (London: Earthscan Publications, 1993), p. 8.
3 UNDP, *Human Development Report 1992* (New York: Oxford University Press, 1992), pp. 34–6.
4 Barbara Ehrenreich, 'Helping America's rich stay that way', *Time* (18 April 1994), p. 76.
5 In *Voyager*, in-flight magazine of British Midland (March/April 1994), p. 29.
6 Paul Hawken, *The Ecology of Commerce: A Declaration of Sustainability* (New York: HarperCollins, 1993), p. 151.
7 Ibid.
8 'Even among the well-off, the richest get richer', *New York Times* (5 March 1992).
9 Conor Clery, 'Jobs, poverty figures will tell against Bush', *Irish Times* (5 September 1992).
10 Andrew Glyn and David Millband, 'Why unequal Britain is paying the price for new Right's "efficiency" fallacy', *Guardian* (25 April 1994), p. 13. The article is a summary of pertinent data from their book *Paying for Inequality: The Economic Cost of Social Injustice* (London: Rivers Oram Press/Institute for Public Policy Research, 1994).
11 David Gow, 'More than 7m Germans "live in poverty" ', *Guardian* (21 January 1994).
12 'EU support launches Delors job scheme', *Guardian* (13 December 1993).
13 Susan George, *The Debt Boomerang* (London: Pluto Press, 1992).
14 *The State of The World's Children*, UNICEF Report (1990).

CHAPTER 2

Unequal trading:
the GATT agreement

ANOTHER INTERNATIONAL MECHANISM – this time in the domain of trade – will adversely affect Third World peoples and the environment. The General Agreement on Tariffs and Trade (GATT) was set up in 1948 with 23 countries participating. Its purpose is to provide a set of mutually agreed rules on the conduct of international trade based on contracts between sovereign states. By attempting to reduce tariffs and other barriers to trade GATT aims to increase the volume of international trade. GATT is more an agreement than a formal organization, unlike the World Bank or the IMF, though that is set to change with the establishment of the World Trade Organization (WTO).

Three principles – non-discrimination, reciprocity, and transparency – form the bedrock of GATT. Non-discrimination means that if a contracting party to GATT wishes to impose a duty on imports from one country it has to apply the same duty to all countries. Reciprocity demands that when a country lowers its tariffs on another country's exports it requires the other country to lower its tariffs in return. Finally, the transparency principle advocates the replacement of non-tariff barriers like quotas with tariffs, because these are easier to monitor.

The earlier seven rounds of GATT negotiations concentrated on reducing tariffs (taxes and duties) and non-tariffs (quotas and import restrictions). The Uruguay Round, completed on 17 December 1993, was fundamentally different. It attempted to incorporate into GATT areas like agriculture, services, foreign investments and intellectual properties. This round was launched at the insistence of the US in response to lobbying by US-based Transnational Corporations (TNCs) to extend the scope of trade agreements beyond goods to include these areas.

The guiding philosophy of most TNCs is to promote low commodity prices and wages, minimum government interference with market forces, and unencumbered access to worldwide markets. The GATT agreement provided the freedom and auto-nomy for TNCs to pursue their goal of greater profits. TNCs wield enormous economic and political power and have come to domin-ate world trade in the past few decades. Dr Kevin Watkins of Oxfam estimates that 70 per cent of world trade is now controlled by TNCs. Much of that trade, possibly up to 40 per cent, is carried out within TNCs. Dr Watkins writes:

> Traditionally, international trade is seen as an activity carried out between nations. In reality, trade flows are dominated by powerful corporations located overwhelmingly in Western Europe, North America and Japan. In 1985, the combined sales of the world's largest TNCs exceeded $3 trillion, equivalent to one-third of the world's Gross Domestic Product [GDP].[1]

SERVING THE STRONGEST

Many Third World people saw the Uruguay Round as an attempt by the US, through US-based corporations, to regain its pre-eminence as the world's economic superpower. In the past decade and a half a significant proportion of worldwide manufacturing capacity has moved to low-wage countries, especially in the Pacific Rim. In response, the US has attempted to protect its economic position through promoting a trading system which will serve its interests in sophisticated computer technology, biotechnology, financial ser-vices, telecommunications and the media. A letter from President Clinton to Congress, in December 1993, which accompanied an executive summary of the Uruguay Round, claimed that 'the Uruguay Round results will provide an unprecedented level of new market access opportunities for US goods and sevices exports'. In almost every sector – beginning with agriculture, where it hoped to increase market share; to textiles and clothing, where it wished to protect its own industry by slowing down the phasing in of the Multi-Fibre Arrangement (MFA) – the US achieved most of the goals which it set in 1986 at the outset of the Uruguay Round.

Undoubtedly, the Uruguay Round will bring a few minor concessions to Third World countries. Third World textile producers want to see the phasing out of the Multi-Fibre Arrangement (MFA). This was established in 1974, with the agreement of GATT, to protect textile producers in rich countries from competition from Third World countries. The final text of GATT agreed to phase out the Arrangement over a period of ten years. However, the small print is more revealing: the phasing-out process will only begin to really hurt the Northern producers from 2002 onwards.

Though 117 countries were involved in the GATT negotiations, supposedly on an equal footing, in fact most of the discussions centred around trade and tariff conflicts between the big players – the US, the EU and Japan. The conflict between the US and Japan was focused on the US–Japan trade deficit, while subsidies for agriculture were the main bone of contention between the US and the EU. These conflicts dominated the final weeks of tense negotiations and sidelined most of the other nations.

It is interesting to compare the Northern countries' rhetoric on free trade with their track record. During the 1980s Northern governments and financial institutions protected themselves against competition from the Third World behind a barricade of tariffs and quotas.[2] They also set about consolidating three large trading blocs. The North American Free Trade Agreement (NAFTA) is dominated by the US, the European Union is dominated by Germany, and Japan is the economic superpower of Asia. So, while these governments were singing the praises of free trade they were busy setting up their own economic safe havens.[3] However, when Southern countries attempt to protect their people and environments they are lectured on the virtues of free trade by Northern politicians or financial institutions.

While the rich countries sparred and attempted to secure advantages for their own economies the development needs of the Two-Thirds World were not addressed in the Uruguay Round of GATT. Proponents of GATT believe that economic progress is only achievable through export-oriented growth, low wages and environmental degradation. Little thought was given to policies that reduce poverty, promote equitable distribution of wealth, sustainable development, environmental protection and self-reliance, especially in the area of food production. The twin millstones of foreign debt and falling commodity prices were effectively ignored. What most poor countries need are economic, agricultural and environmental policies which are sustainable, meet the needs of the poor, and facilitate self-reliance, full employment, social security and popular participation.[4]

The concerns of the Two-Thirds World were barely heard at GATT. The sweep of the negotiations and the technical complexities involved placed most Third World countries in a very invidious position. Very few had the technical expertise or the continuity of personnel, at government or civil servant level, to monitor the process and effectively challenge the hegemony of Northern countries. Disunity also marred any attempt by the South to develop alternative strategies which would help all poor countries. Some natural leaders among the Southern bloc, like India and Brazil, initially resisted Northern moves towards the Uruguay Round. However, as the negotiations proceeded they bargained to achieve concessions and access to Northern markets and eschewed any responsibility for wider Southern concerns.

The North held out the carrot of world trade expansion to the level of $200 billion a year (based on an OECD study) to persuade the Two-Thirds World to sign up to the GATT agreement. The improved performance in Northern economies, so the argument went, would stimulate demand and open up more markets for products from the South. This conventional wisdom maintains that a global trading system which encourages the increase of global production is beneficial to all trading partners. Who could be against this presumed win–win situation for everyone? Moreover free trade, like freedom of speech, seems so desirable that no one who cherishes freedom could be opposed to it.

Terminology, however, can easily mislead and obfuscate an issue. A more accurate name for 'free trade' is 'deregulated international markets'. Deregulation is not always desirable. In the United States, in the early 1980s, the deregulation of the Savings and Loans institutions almost led to the collapse of the financial system.[5]

The overwhelming advantages of free trade, according to the neo-classical economic theory, are based on the dogma of comparative advantage. The doctrine of comparative advantage proposes that individual countries, because of either climate, mineral resources or the skills of the work force, enjoy a special advantage in a given area of agricultural or industrial production. At the time of David Ricardo who articulated the doctrine, Portugal had a comparative advantage in wine production over England whereas it worked the other way in the case of textiles. According to this theory it made economic sense for England to import wine and export textiles. However, it is often forgotten by modern proponents of free trade that, as stated by Ricardo, comparative advantage rested on the assumption that capital and labour do not move across national boundaries. It is only when capital is not free to move to another country that there is any pressure on it to specialize within a country according to the dictates of the principle of comparative advantage. In the present economic situation in which capital, goods and labour are constantly on the move in international markets, capital seeks absolute advantage by moving to the low-cost country. There is little incentive to seek a special niche within a given country and invest there when huge profits can be made elsewhere.[6] Secondly, in the context of the development debate the pro-GATT rhetoric also involves recycling the old, discredited 'trickle-down' theory which claims that a larger economic pie will help everyone. The statistics in Chapter 1 show that this does not happen: the poor, in fact, get poorer.

Many people concerned with development or environment issues would agree with the views which Professor D. A. Turner of the University of Kent expressed in a letter to the *Guardian* (17 December 1993). He wrote that the GATT agreement is 'a victory for the agenda of greedy and short-sighted multinationals who seek to maximize their profits regardless of the human and social cost'. But what, exactly, does the GATT agreement entail? And why should the areas covered by the Uruguay Round – intellectual properties, services and agriculture, for example – prove to be so contentious for the South?

TRIPS – THE NEW COLONIALISM?

In the long term, the provisions on Trade-related Intellectual Property Rights (TRIPs) will probably do the most damage to Southern countries. This is particularly true in agriculture, where TRIPs constitute a threat to farmers' rights to their seeds and animals. Once these are patented by corporations the farmers will have to pay royalties for both the seeds and the offspring, as the reproductive capacity will remain the property of the patent owner.

Intellectual Property Rights (IPRs) such as patents are designed to protect inventions or products of human ingenuity. A patent gives an individual or corporation monopoly rights to use an invention for a set period of time. The purpose of patents is to compensate the inventor for the time, energy and money spent developing a new product. Until recently, patent legislation was confined to inanimate objects and living matter was excluded. The legislation also attempted to balance two sets of rights: the right of the inventor to proper compensation, and the equally important right of the public to benefit from the fruits of intellectual research.

In the Uruguay Round of GATT, however, the US government – spurred on by its biotechnological and pharmaceutical companies – widened the notion of intellectual properties. Previous conventions on patenting, like the 1883 Paris Convention and the 1886 Berne Convention (updated in 1948), recognized that individual countries had particular needs and priorities and that this would have to be reflected in the way patent legislation was formulated. Given the diverse codes of practice, it was agreed that patents registered in one country should only be applicable there.

However, in recent years, many US corporations have accused Third World countries of pirating US patents and thereby engaging in 'unfair trading practices'. In order to rectify this the US used the Uruguay Round to force Third World countries to incorporate the narrow, US-inspired perception of IPRs in their domestic legislation. This change favours the interests of TNCs rather than the requirements of the common good. Inevitably it will lead to intellectual and cultural impoverishment and a built-in dependence of Third World agriculture and medicine on First World corporations.

The preamble to the GATT TRIPs agreement acknowledges that IPRs are recognized only as private rights. Knowledge and ideas which originate in the 'intellectual commons' are excluded from consideration. This 'commons' refers, for example, to the pool of shared knowledge in the field of seed or animal breeding which has been passed on, over centuries, by peasant farmers, tribal people or even publicly funded scientific research.

The patenting of oil products derived from the neem tree is a case in point. For generations Indian farmers and traditional physicians have used a variety of products derived from this tree. The bark, flowers, seeds and fruit pulp are used to treat diseases ranging from leprosy to diabetes and ulcers. Its potential to rehabilitate exhausted soils was recognized in ancient Sanskrit texts. This versatile tree also plays a role in animal husbandry: neem cake is often fed to livestock and poultry. In addition, solutions derived from neem are an effective insecticide against locusts, plant-hoppers, Colorado beetles and boll weevils, amongst others. Little wonder then that the neem tree has been celebrated by Indian people down through the centuries. In ancient Sanskrit text the tree is called *sarva roga nivarini* (the curer of all ailments), while Indian Muslims referred to it as *shajar-e-mubarak* (the blessed tree).

Until recently the technologies to extract the various oils from the tree were simple and cheap, which meant that ordinary people could benefit from its bounty. No individual or company in India attempted to acquire proprietary ownership over the neem proper-ties as, under Indian law, agricultural and medicinal products are not patentable. Since 1985, however, a number of US and Japanese companies have taken out over a dozen US-based patents on formulae for stable neem-based solutions and emulsions. Indian farmers and politicians have objected to foreign TNCs garnering the fruits of centuries of care lavished on this tree by generations of Indians who helped develop techniques to make its beneficial properties available to all people.[7]

This US-led patent control is not confined to India. The University of Toledo, for example, has filed a patent claim on endod, commonly known as the soapberry plant. It has been used both as a shampoo and as an effective treatment for schistosomiasis, a debilitating disease which afflicts many people in the tropics. Another US-based TNC, Levi-Strauss (the worldwide jeans manu-facturer), holds a patent for a variety of cotton seeds that are naturally coloured. These seeds originated in Bolivia and were cultivated, over the centuries, by the peoples of the Andes. Since the patent is held in the US it has become illegal to grow the traditional varieties in Bolivia.[8]

Undoubtedly GATT patent legislation will benefit the rich North. Less than 5 per cent of the world's 30 million or so patents originate in the South, and the majority of those are held by Northern TNCs. Moreover, it is often forgotten that patent legislation was less restrictive when many of today's First World countries were attempting to industrialize and develop.

According to article 27.1 of the GATT text, an innovation must be capable of industrial application to be recognized as an intellectual property. The positive side of this stipulation is that it is designed to ensure that a patentee cannot keep a potentially useful invention out of the public domain. The negative side is that the profit motive is the overriding concern in patent legislation. The ongoing debates in many countries regarding patented or generic drugs illustrate that a lengthy patent period does not serve the interests of the vast majority of people, especially the poor. In India, for example, current intellectual properties legislation means that many drugs are available for a fraction of what they cost in First World countries. It has been estimated that the new GATT rules would increase the cost of medicines sharply in most of the Two-Thirds World. In some instances the increase could be around 500 per cent.

In Argentina, for example, US trade negotiators (at the behest of drug companies) are trying to force the government to adopt patent policies that could triple the price of drug prescriptions. The anti-ulcer medication Zantac, which costs $91.98 in the US, costs $18.17 in Argentina.[9] If the Argentine government is forced, by the threat of economic sanctions, to modify its existing patent laws the result will be a much poorer health care service and a huge drain in resources as royalties are paid to foreign TNCs.

The GATT text further states in article 27.5.3 that 'parties may exclude from patentability plants and animals . . . '. However, the next sentence effectively nullifies this exclusion by stating that 'protection of plant varieties [must be achieved] either by patents or by an effective *sui generis* system or by any combination thereof'. Moreover, the initial exclusion does not embrace the possibility of patenting parts of genetically altered plants, animals or micro-organisms. Many people share the fear expressed by the Indian scientist Vandana Shiva that this is the 'beginning of a journey down the slippery slope that leads to the patenting of all life'.[10]

This protection of plant varieties will have an immediate effect on farmers in the Two-Thirds World. Third World governments will have to introduce GATT-like legislation. Their farmers will be forced to pay royalties for all their seeds which could drive many subsistence farmers off the land, a prospect which has alarmed a number of Third World farming organizations. In late 1992 the Karnataka Farmers Union in southern India protested against GATT's patent proposals by ransacking the Bangalore office of the giant agribusiness corporation, Cargill Seeds. Further large-scale demonstrations took place in India in March and October 1993. In April 1994 more than 100,000 people gathered in Delhi to oppose the GATT agreement, especially the provisions on IPRs.[11]

Many people argue that the patenting of living tissue should be excluded from a multilateral trade agreement like GATT. The debate surrounding the patenting of living matter is not primarily about trade or economics; it concerns much deeper ethical, religious and ecological questions, such as how human beings should relate to other creatures on the planet. Many ethicists question whether human beings have the right to genetically engineer animals to produce extra milk or leaner meat, especially when the end result causes structural and physiological problems to the animals. They argue that animals are not machines to be manipulated to satisfy human whims and greed, they are sentient beings who have their own integrity. For this reason a group of independent scientists from the International Biotechnology Network have recommended that article 27.3(b) of GATT be redrafted to exclude all living organisms, thus ensuring that life is not turned into a patentable commodity to increase corporate profits.

MEDIA IMPERIALISM

The Uruguay Round of the General Agreement on Trade in Services (GATS) also poses problems for Third World countries. Some fear that this agreement will facilitate the expansion of Northern media companies into the Third World. The acquisition of the Star satellite TV company in Hong Kong by Rupert Murdoch sent warning lights flashing in other Asian countries. The Malaysian Prime Minister Mahathir Mohamad wondered whether Murdoch was intent on controlling the news in Asia since he was willing to spend $500 million on a station that has never shown a profit.[12]

Trade in audio-visuals was one of the services covered in the Uruguay Round and the discussion envisaged the transborder delivery of these services. The Thai journalist Chakravarthi Raghavan argues that 'If countries in Asia agree to "liberalize" this sector in their initial commitments on services in trade to permit transborder delivery, then service providers like Star TV can get a legal foothold, expand their markets in each of the countries involved, and would be guaranteed earnings and repatriation of earnings'.[13]

The present text of the agreement poses particular problems in Southeast Asia. In a country like the Philippines the élite, who have substantial spending power, use English as a second language. They will be a ready target for external media giants like Murdoch or Ted Turner of Cable News Network (CNN). Local governments who may wish to promote their own cultures will be prohibited from legislating for a certain percentage of programmes beamed to a particular country to be produced locally. Given the availability of technology to deliver transborder services it is important that the rules of the International Telecommunications Union (ITU) be strengthened to protect small and vulnerable cultures and countries from media imperialism.

Commercial considerations could also lead to censoring news. Writing in the *Guardian* (1 April 1994), David Mellor calls attention to a fundamental inconsistency in Mr Murdoch's stance towards uncensored access to news. Mr Murdoch was quoted in *The Times* (7 September 1993) as saying that satellite television had helped overthrow the Marxist regimes in Europe by making it possible for 'many information-hungry residents of many closed societies to bypass state-controlled television'. Four months later he bowed to political pressure from China and withdrew BBC World Service News from his television channel Star TV. As Mellor comments, 'so much for Murdoch's commitment to beam free news into totalitarian countries'.

THREATS TO THE ENVIRONMENT AND SOCIETY

Many sustainable development programmes in the South, which are protected by government subsidies, might also be declared in breach of GATT regulations. In 1982, for example, Costa Rica was forced to dismantle its support system for small farmers as a precondition for receiving US aid. As a result thousands of farmers became bankrupt and had to leave the land. Many moved to the shanty towns of the cities in search of work, adding to the pressures on already overstretched services. Others moved to the perimeter of the rainforest. In order to feed their families they engaged in slash-and-burn agriculture and thus increased the forest's destruction. In a similar vein, economists estimate that the removal of protection for Mexican corn and other food items under NAFTA and the tariff-free entry of low-price US grain will significantly affect Mexican farming. Professor D. A. Turner estimates that the GATT deal will drive about 40 per cent of the 2 billion subsistence farmers worldwide off the land. 'Anyone who thinks that the cities of the Third World, already teeming with misery, unemployment and child prostitution, can absorb another 800 million ruined peasants is substituting the ideological dogmas of the New Right for serious thought.'[14]

The lack of environmental consciousness in the present provisions of GATT can even work against environmental legislation in First World countries. In 1990 the US banned the import of Mexican tuna because the fishing nets used by Mexican trawlers also killed an excessive number of dolphins, thereby contravening the 1972 US Marine Protection Act (amended in 1988). The GATT panel found that the US tuna ban contravened GATT provisions and therefore constituted a discriminatory trade measure. A private Greenpeace briefing paper in December 1993 stated that 'despite some concerns about the fairness of the relationship between US laws and Mexican fishermen, the precedent set by this GATT decision was seen by a wide range of US environmental, conservation and animal protection organizations as a direct threat to their efforts to promote sustainable trade and simultaneous conservation'.

A foretaste of the social and ecological effects of untrammelled free trade can already be seen along the 1,250-mile border between Mexico and the US. Even before the completion of NAFTA or the Uruguay Round of GATT, hundreds of foreign companies established almost 2,000 subsidiary factories (*maquiladoras*) there. The reasons are simple: low wages, non-existent or ineffective unions, poor environmental legislation and Mexico's lax environmental enforcement.

The human and environmental costs of this development are enormous. In Mexican border towns like Matamoros workers are paid a pittance. The average wage in a local automobile plant ranges from $4 to $10 per day, while a worker in a similar plant in the US earns between $10 and $15 per hour. Workers at the Mexican plants work in a highly polluted environment and are also often exposed to dangerous chemicals and toxic substances. Peter Lennon, writing in the *Guardian* (21 August 1992), describes how both the Mexican and United States governments have tacitly agreed to 'disregard the safeguards workers have won over the century and deny protection to the environment in the name of "economic progress" and a free-trade agreement'. The effects have been frightening. More than 40 anencephalic (brainless) babies have been born in the area during the past two years. The streets of Matamoros are full of calcium sulphate and hydrofluoric acid, and it is estimated that it will cost around $9 billion to clean it up.

The same trend is visible in Europe. Companies are moving from high-wage countries like France and Germany to eastern Europe, where wages are often one-tenth of what they are in western Europe and environmental protection is weak. Corporations are threatening to move to low-wage countries to depress wages in Europe and the US. Richard Rothstein of the Economic Policy Institute estimates that during the 1980s this threat reduced wages in the US by an average of 10 per cent.[15]

GATT officials appear not to see much need to address environmental issues urgently. Peter Sutherland, the present Director-General of GATT, indicated that he might look at 'the environment' once the Uruguay Round was completed. Considering that the Uruguay Round took seven years to complete, companies that pollute will be secure in the knowledge that they have effectively buried any competitors who might be concerned about environmental protection, before any agreed environmental directives take hold. Effective mechanisms to force industry to internalize environmental costs should have been a factor in the Uruguay Round. Without these there are no incentives to invest in conservation programmes and new, environmentally friendly, clean technology.

Finally, and most significant of all, few people have considered the 'economic growth' rhetoric of GATT. How can continual economic growth be achieved in a finite world without destroying the environment? Environmental economics challenges the wisdom and assumptions of neo-classical economic theory and the dogma of comparative advantage. It insists that the human economy is a subsystem of a larger, finite, non-expanding earth. Human economic activity cannot continue to expand exponentially, especially when that means running down, often irreversibly, the ecological capital of a country or the world as a whole. Environmental economics argues that ecological goods are not free and that man-made capital cannot always be substituted for ecological capital.

Environmental economics calls attention to the limits that exist at both the source and sink side of the equation. *Source* limits relate to the ability of biological systems to regenerate themselves, and also the use of non-renewable energy and resources. *Sink* limits focus on the ability of a particular ecosystem, or the earth as a whole, to absorb the impact of human-generated pollution. Sooner or later human economic systems must adapt to a pattern of development which does not necessitate a growth in throughput.

In an attempt to deal with Green criticism of GATT, a working group was set up in December 1993 to examine ways to inject environmental considerations into GATT's successor, the World Trade Organization (WTO). This organization will effectively become the world's trade policeman when it takes over the role of

GATT in 1995. As the environment did not figure prominently during the seven years of the Uruguay Round, environmentalists are sceptical that the working party will achieve anything substantial. Some see it merely as a public relations exercise to blunt criticism of the agreement from the Green lobby. Unless the principles of environmental economics are taken into consideration, it is unlikely that anything much will change.

THIRD WORLD AGRICULTURE

GATT apologists claim that the agricultural provisions will improve Third World agriculture by reducing both domestic support and export subsidies, which promote over-production and dumping. The measures appear to be weighted in favour of Third World countries: reducing domestic support by only 13.3 per cent over ten years, while the 'developed' countries are required to reduce theirs by 20 per cent in six years. On the export side, Northern subsidies are to be reduced by 36 per cent while Southern countries are only required to make cuts of 24 per cent. It sounds like a good deal, but it is not the whole picture.

The ruling on domestic support does not apply to what is termed 'delinked' payments. This refers to payments which are not connected directly to the level of farm output like the income support system in Europe and the deficiency payment scheme in the US. The editors of *The Ecologist* insist that 'in effect, these are export subsidies under another name, which enable the grain companies to "buy cheap" and thus to undercut competitors in foreign markets'.[16] The big beneficiaries are not the people of the Third World or even the family farmers of the North but a handful of transnational agribusiness corporations like Continental Grain, Cargill, Louis Dreyfus, Mitsui/Cook and Pioneer, Dole, and Del Monte.

TNCs will also benefit from the exemption on domestic agricultural subsidies. While Southern governments will not be able to subsidize seeds, fertilizers, marketing or credit for subsistence farmers, they will be allowed to subsidize what are termed 'marketing and promotion services'. This translates into roads, irrigation systems and other infrastructural work, most of which will benefit large corporations who deal in export crops like bananas, pineapple and sugar. It will not substantially help family farmers gain better access to local markets.

The figures on market access for Third World countries are also revealing. At first glance they appear like a good deal for the South. Third World countries must open at least 2 per cent of their domestic food markets to foreign sources. Within ten years this figure must rise to 3.3 per cent. The Northern threshold begins at 3 per cent and must jump to 5 per cent. However, given the huge populations in the South, 2 per cent of Third World markets represents a much larger base than 3 per cent of Northern markets. Furthermore, agriculture represents 18 per cent of Tanzania's GNP, for example, and only 0.5 per cent of the US's GNP. So, the 2 per cent penetration by foreign-sourced food is much larger than a 3 per cent slice of the US economy.

Northern agricultural exports to Southern countries involve staple foodstuffs, expecially grains. There is a great danger that Southern countries will become dependent on substantial imports to provide staple food for their people. This is a recipe for malnutrition and famine. Given the history of Ireland's Great Famine in the 1840s, people should be alarmed that GATT forbids the imposition of bans on the export of food even when there is a shortage on the domestic front. It is also important to emphasize that these agricultural policies leave Southern countries extremely vulnerable to political manipulation from the North. The threat of cutting off the food supply would bring any Southern government to its knees. A similar danger does not exist in the South-to-North flow of agricultural goods since the exports from Southern countries are primarily luxury crops, e.g. mangoes or baby corn. Nobody will starve if they have to forgo these.[17]

While there will be a few benefits to Southern countries from reductions in agricultural subsidies, especially in the EU, the long-term impact of the Uruguay Round on the Two-Thirds World's agriculture and economies will be disastrous. Their ability to pursue independent economic policies, responsive primarily to the needs of their own people, will be severely curtailed. GATT, in its present form, will extend and tighten the control of TNCs on Southern economies. Third World governments, for example, will no longer be able to require TNCs to use a certain percentage of local technology or materials in industrial processes. The well-being of Third World people would also be much better served if GATT recognized that food security was a desirable goal for each country. This would mean developing agricultural policies whereby countries grow their own basic food, taking into account their climate, nutritional needs and food culture.

The drive for globalization, powered by free trade and the effect of market forces, also means that Northern countries are losing the freedom to design their economic systems so that these undergird cherished cultural values. In the *Guardian* John Gray upbraids the New Right for promoting a process of globalization which is seriously undermining community life in Britain. He argues that it is necessary to 'oppose the desolation wrought on communities by policies that have no justification apart from the spurious claim that they are forced on us by an inexorable historical process'.[18]

A CALL FOR IMPROVED CONDITIONS

The much vaunted international competitiveness which many countries are trying to attain ought not to be achieved at the expense of workers' wages, health or safety. Unfortunately, this trend has been discernible for over a decade. Since 1982, for example, the purchasing power of wages in Mexico has fallen by around 60 per cent. This is a direct result of the economic policies pursued by the Mexican government. It promoted a growth strategy which relied on fostering low wages in order to achieve comparative advantage on international markets. Many companies, especially those involved in export-oriented industries, have achieved increased competitiveness through hiring part-time workers or securing temporary contracts.

Even in the United States, part-time work has now become a permanent feature of employment for many people. This sector is one of the fastest growing areas of the economy. The choices for many people are stark: either accept a low-paid job with no benefits or job security, or remain unemployed.

To avoid the present downward pressure towards starvation levels on wages GATT, or any multilateral trade agreement, must enshrine procedures which protect the rights of workers to organize freely, to join unions and to engage in collective bargaining. The minimum standard for the protection of workers, which is laid down by the International Labour Organization (ILO), should be incorporated into any agreement. It must also insist on high health and safety standards and adequate insurance for workers.

GATT also should have incorporated strict environmental guidelines. At the moment many international environmental agreements, like the Montreal Protocol on the Ozone Layer, and national environmental legislation, for example the US's Endangered

Species Act, are undermined by GATT rulings. The GATT panel decided that the agreement prevents countries from taking trade measures to protect the environment or natural resources beyond their national boundaries. The judgement eliminates the possibility of threatening economic sanctions to protect unique habitats. The effect of this on international treaties could be disastrous.

Furthermore, domestic environment or food safety legislation could easily be undermined. If a country with stringent standards for pesticide use decided to restrict the importation of foods with higher levels of pesticides that country could be sued for establishing non-tariff barriers to trade. This could affect the UK's rules on labelling irradiated food, Denmark's ban on PVC food containers, and Germany's law on recycling beverage containers. The pressure to lower standards in food safety is illustrated by the call to adopt the food standards set by the Codex Alimentarius in Rome. Present Codex rules would allow, for example, the importation of bananas into the US with 50 times more DDT residue than that allowed by the US Food and Drug Administration. A nation with higher food safety standards could be required to prove to a GATT panel that their higher standards were based on 'scientific principles'.

Environmental imperatives call for a much more decentralized economic system with a much greater degree of local control. This is anathema to those who subscribe to the neo-liberal economic philosophy enshrined in the GATT agreement. Out of the 2,019 delegates who attended the Codex meetings from 1989 to 1991, 445 represented industry and over half of the US and Swiss government delegates came from food and agrochemical companies. A mere eight delegates represented non-government organizations (NGOs) or citizens groups. The Third World was dramatically underrepresented: 7 per cent came from Africa and 10 per cent from Latin America. Little wonder then that the people fear many of the decisions of the Codex will be weighed in favour of industry.[19]

NEED TO INTERNALIZE ENVIRONMENTAL COSTS AND PROMOTE SUSTAINABILITY

Effective mechanisms must be found to force industry to internalize environmental costs. Prices and production costs must reflect the cost of waste disposal, pollution clean-up and other remedial and preventative measures. Industries must not be allowed to transfer the adverse effects of their extraction or production from countries which have strict environmental laws to those where they are non-existent or lax in implementation. A report on the Taiwanese environment, *Taiwan 2000*, recognizes that lack of environmental legislation was a factor in luring industry to Taiwan during the past 30 years:

> Because weak environmental regulation has given Taiwan a competitive advantage for polluting industries, hazardous waste sources have grown relatively rapidly in Taiwan and can be expected to do so . . . The competitive advantage of an unregulated island may also draw other industries that confront stiff environmental regulations in other industrialized areas, including industries involved with some high-risk forms of biotechnology.[20]

This kind of comparative advantage should not be rewarded in a multilateral trading agreement. There is a major difference between traditional forms of protectionism, whereby tariffs or quotas are used to protect inefficient industries, and the use of tariffs to protect against dumping by countries with a deplorable social and environmental record. The latter may be the only sensible way to foster an effective national environmental policy which requires environmental costs to be fully internalized.

It should be recognized that trading agreements can be used to promote clean and energy-efficient technologies. The three giant United States automobile corporations were forced to improve the fuel efficiency of their cars because of stiff competition from Japanese car manufacturers. Rather than acting to lower environmental standards agreements should move toward higher codes of practice by enunciating bench-marks below which no member state ought to be allowed to fall. Harmonization rules, for example in the Codex Alimentarius, should be moving up rather than down the scale of protection.

On a broader front, any multilateral trading agreement should seek to promote the principles of sustainable development which were enunciated at the United Nations Conference on Environment and Development (UNCED) held in Rio in 1992. UNCED recognized that 'international trade and environmental policies must be mutually supportive in favour of sustainable development'.

Governments recognized the importance of sustainable development and committed themselves to promoting this through organizations like GATT; however, little was done to make the Uruguay
Round environmentally friendly.

The long-term goal of economic planning and trading policies
should be to achieve as much local and regional self-reliance as
possible. It is estimated that one-eighth of the world's oil consumption is used in transporting goods in international trade, and this
does not include the fuel used in transporting goods by road or rail.
A dramatic increase in world trade will automatically mean using
more non-renewable fossil fuels, which contribute significantly to
such environmental ills as global warming and acid rain. Policies
that foster the production of goods and services at local, regional or
national level should be promoted, thus lessening the need to
transport goods across the world unnecessarily.[21]

GATT needs to be transformed radically in order to take on
board these social and ecological concerns. In its present form it will
lead to a lowering of wages, a decline in workers' conditions and a
drop in environmental standards worldwide. It would appear that
Kenneth Clarke, British Chancellor of the Exchequer at the time of
writing, would like to see this trend continue. At a meeting of the
policy-making committee of the IMF in April 1994 he warned of too
much Green concern in discussions about trade agreements. He
also said that the World Trade Organization (WTO) should resist
pressures to enforce minimum labour standards in member states.[22]

It is against this kind of background that the authors of *The New
Protectionism* favour a General Agreement on Sustainable Trade
(GAST). Member countries would be encouraged to constantly
improve standards and the norms governing harmonization in the
areas of safety, working conditions and environmental protection,
providing a floor below which no country would be allowed to
descend.[23]

Finally, many of the present GATT procedures take place behind
closed doors. Like the Codex Alimentarius they are more responsive to industries' needs than to the concerns of either Third World
peoples or consumer or citizen groups in the First World. Such
bodies are non-democratic and non-transparent. The GATT dispute settlement process must be made more transparent and
accountable. It must be open to representatives of interested
parties, including personnel from non-government development
and environmental organizations and citizens groups.

THE WORLD TRADE ORGANIZATION (WTO)

The World Trade Organization (WTO) will succeed GATT in 1995. The WTO, as a new global trade-regulating organization, will greatly expand the role of GATT. The WTO will ensure that member countries comply with the decisions embodied in the rules of trade agreed in the Uruguay Round. It will also put pressure on domestic governments to bring domestic laws and regulations into line with GATT, which will undoubtedly have a very negative impact on many poor countries.

The WTO will contain a Dispute Settlement Understanding (DSU) unit for disputes which arise between members over the various agreements within the GATT text. If a member country does not carry out its obligations and is found in breach by the DSU, then a trading partner can retaliate. The US has been using such threats in recent years to force its tobacco products into various Asian markets (under the notorious Section 301 of the US Trade Law). Most poor countries, because they are dependent on one or two commodities, will not be in a position to retaliate.

It also seems clear that the WTO will have a structure similar to that of the World Bank and the IMF. This is a cause of concern for many Southern commentators and Northern development and environment agencies as neither of these bodies has a good record in promoting poverty alleviation or environmental well-being. While recently they have begun to talk about defeating poverty and promoting sustainable development their track record is poor. It is not clear how the WTO will co-operate with United Nations agencies like UNCTAD (the UN Commission on Trade and Development) or the Commission for Sustainable Development, however it does envisage working closely with the IMF and the World Bank.

Both the IMF and the World Bank are lacking in participation, transparency of operations and accountable procedures. If the WTO is patterned on these institutions it will be ominous for weaker countries to have such a powerful international organization dominated by Northern personnel and financial interests. The obsession with secrecy was reflected in the way the WTO was formulated. The draft text, produced in secret, raises questions about how a body with enormous powers to intervene and regulate world trade, intellectual rights and production patterns will be held accountable. Many Third World NGOs are wary of the text, as the 'development principle' – which recognizes and responds to the special needs of Third World countries – is scaled down considerably.

Instead of concentrating enormous economic power in the hands of fewer and fewer people who operate in remote institutions every effort must be made to return power to local level. Only at the local level can people actually be held accountable by anything resembling the democratic process. The bottom line is that unless a multilateral trade agreement promotes social equality and environmental protection the crisis which the global 'commons' faces will continue to escalate.

In his 1991 encyclical *Centesimus Annus* (*100 Years of Catholic Social Teaching*) Pope John Paul II, while giving a limited endorsement to a certain form of capitalism, calls for a 'strong juridical framework which places it [the business economy] at the service of human freedom in its totality' (no. 42). He also recognizes the need for 'adequate intervention at the international level' (no. 52) to ensure that the system works equitably. He acknowledges that this 'may mean making important changes in established lifestyles, in order to limit the waste of environmental and human resources, thus enabling every individual and all the peoples of the earth to have a sufficient share of those resources' (no. 52). This call for a wider juridical framework is based on the realization that trade is such a complex reality in the modern world. It impinges on so many other aspects of both human life and the environment that no single institution can address all the relevant issues.

For this reason a multilateral trading organization will need clear and formal institutional links with other United Nations organizations and NGOs. Matters related to working conditions, minimum wages and migrant labour must be tackled in conjunction with the ILO. Environmental considerations should involve the UN Commission for Sustainable Development. The dominant role of TNCs should be closely monitored through special UN agencies devoted to this work. Unfortunately, the United Nations agency which studied and monitored TNCs – the UN Centre for Transnational Corporations – was scaled down dramatically in 1992 after the Rio Summit. (Many people believe this was the result of powerful lobbying by TNCs, who wished to scuttle over a decade's work on the Code of Conduct on TNCs.) Given the economic power of such giant corporations there is a need for some form of International Monopolies and Mergers Commission with the powers and resources to break up these powerful cartels. At present there is no regulatory framework to monitor their formidable power. Many of the thorny questions involved in TRIPs – especially as they impinge on food, agriculture and medicine – should be decided in conjunction with the UN organizations like the World Health Organization (WHO) and the Food and Agriculture Organization (FAO). Poor and vulnerable nations could expect more sympathetic treatment from such organizations.[24]

* * *

The 400-page main text and the 18,000 pages of detailed agreements of the Uruguay Round of GATT were signed by over 110 countries at a meeting of Trade Ministers in Marrakesh on 15 April 1994. This cleared the way for the setting up the WTO on 1 January 1995. The dream of the participants at the international conference in 1944 of setting up three institutions – the World Bank, the International Monetary Fund and the World Trade Organization – will at last have come to pass.

A letter in the *Guardian* (15 April 1994), signed by both Ian Linden of the Catholic Institute for International Relations in London and Luis Hernandez from the Centre of Studies for Change in Rural Mexico, rightly asserts that the claim that all nations will benefit from the Uruguay Round agreement is a PR sham. 'The World Bank and the OECD's own estimates project that the world's poorest countries will lose.'

NOTES
1 Quoted in Tim Lang and Colin Hines, *The New Protectionism: Protecting the Future Against Free Trade* (London: Earthscan Publications, 1993), p. 34.
2 Ibid., p. 41.
3 Ibid., p. 42.
4 Economic Justice Report, '51 alternatives to NAFTA', *IDOC Internationale* 3.93, p. 39.
5 Herman Daly, 'The perils of free trade', *Scientific American* (November 1993), p. 24.
6 Herman Daly and Robert Goodland, 'An ecological–economic assessment of deregulation and of international commerce under GATT' (World Bank discussion paper, 25 September 1992).
7 Vandana Shiva and Radha Holla-Bhar, 'Intellectual piracy and the neem tree', *The Ecologist*, vol. 23, no. 6 (November/December 1993), pp. 223–7.
8 Uinsionn MacDubhghaill, 'Now no life form is safe from the patent lawyers', *Irish Times* (16 October 1993).
9 Steve Farnswort, 'The drug monopoly', *Multinational Monitor* (November 1993), pp. 11–12.
10 Vandana Shiva, 'Patenting life forms', *Third World Resurgence*, no. 38 (October 1993), pp. 4–5.
11 John Rettle, '100,000 caught in Indian anti-GATT riot', *Guardian* (6 April 1994).

12 Yojana Sharma, 'Western media gain a foothold in Asia', *Third World Resurgence*, no. 37 (September 1993), pp. 33–4.
13 Chakravarthi Raghavan, 'Services accord may further media imperialism', *Third World Resurgence*, no. 37, pp. 37–8.
14 D. A. Turner, letter to the *Guardian* (17 December 1993).
15 Quoted in John Cavanagh et al. (eds), *Trading Freedom* (San Francisco: Institute for Food and Development Policy, 1992) p. 8.
16 'Cakes and caviar? The Dunkel draft and Third World agriculture', *The Ecologist*, vol. 23, no. 6 (November/December 1993), pp. 219–22.
17 Ibid.
18 John Gray, 'Against the world', *Guardian* (4 January 1994).
19 Natalie Avery, Martine Drake and Tim Lang, 'Codex Alimentarius: who is allowed in? Who is left out?', *The Ecologist*, vol. 23, no. 3 (May/June 1993), pp. 110–12.
20 *Taiwan 2000* (Nanking, Taipei: Institute of Ethnology, Academia Sinica, 1989), p. 35.
21 Lang and Hines, op. cit., p. 14.
22 Norman Peter, 'Clarke warns of too much green concern', *Financial Times* (26 April 1994).
23 Lang and Hines, op. cit., p. 130.
24 Leelananda de Silva, *A Curate's Egg: An Assessment of the Multilateral Trade Organization* (London: CAFOD, Christian Aid and Oxfam, October 1993).

CHAPTER 3

Limited
resources

T HE QUESTION of whether there are upper limits to the earth's capacity to cope with human activity was first addressed in a serious way in *Limits to Growth*, published in 1972. The book generated a huge response and sold 10 million copies in all. It comprised a report *for* the Club of Rome rather than *by* the Club of Rome and naturally not everyone was pleased with its conclusions.

It gave rise to many controversies, not least the methodology used and the inaccuracy of some of the predictions, especially those made about the timeframe in which strategic non-renewable resources might be exhausted. Critics argued that the authors did not take human ingenuity sufficiently into account and thus they underestimated the capability of technology to find substitutes for projected scarcities. It was predicted, for example, that the supply of copper would soon run out given the rising demand in the field of telecommunications. The invention of fibre optics changed all that. Fibre optics revolutionized telecommunications and took the pressure off a metal like copper. The price of copper fell, with devastating impact on copper-producing countries like Bolivia and Zambia.

Although technological innovation can initially reduce both raw material and energy use, this may be offset by a sizeable increase in the overall use or quantity of a given item. For example, in the aftermath of the rise in oil prices between 1973 and 1988 there was a marked increase in energy efficiency in cars. Consumption per kilometre fell by 29 per cent. This gain, however, was quickly offset by a 58 per cent increase in the number of cars during the same period. Despite the introduction of energy-efficient cars, petrol consumption increased by 17 per cent.[1]

While there were quibbles with some of the predictions made in *Limits to Growth*, the book's main significance was that it focused people's attention on the fact that the earth is a finite planet that cannot sustain continuous, expanding demands on its resources. The 'limits to growth' perspective challenges one of the main assumptions of present development theory: that the 5.5 billion people on earth in the mid-1990s – and the projected population of 11 billion by 2050 – can aspire to the present affluent standards of living enjoyed by many Northern middle-class people and the élite in the Southern countries. In reality, the present demands which humans make on the earth are already breaching some important limits in the biosphere. Any substantial increase in these demands will exceed the capacity of the larger ecosystems to regenerate themselves. Continuously spiralling demand is simply not possible on a finite planet.

Those commentators who assert that the projected 11 billion people can aspire to 'Western' affluence need to keep two considerations in mind. Firstly, the foundations of Northern prosperity were built on four centuries of colonialism, during which Westerners had control over the resources and the people living in the Two-Thirds World. Thomas Pakenham, in his classic work *The Scramble for Africa*, chronicles the saga of greed and exploitation which was the basic motivation behind the movement of the Western powers into Africa in the second half of the nineteenth century. The greed, venality and brutality which were central to the colonial venture were often cloaked in the lofty sentiments of bringing the three Cs – Commerce, Civilization, and Christianity – to benefit the peoples of Africa.[2]

Secondly, the sizeable spurt in Western economic growth since World War II was achieved when the main source of energy was exceptionally cheap. During this spectacular period of industrial and commercial expansion, between 1945 and 1973, the price of oil was less than $3 a barrel. A handful of Western oil corporations controlled the industry and worked to keep the price as low as possible. At the same time industrialized countries had considerable access to cheap Third World labour and resources.

The notion of 'limits' on a finite planet, therefore, must be recognized and the effects of Northern affluence on food production, biodiversity, air, water and our very long-term survival on earth must be acknowledged. The present imbalances must be redressed, not further promoted.

LIMITS ON FOOD PRODUCTION

Like other organisms, human beings need an adequate intake of nutritious food to survive and thrive. Because of widespread poverty in much of the South many people there do not have a nutritionally adequate diet at the moment. In fact the average person there consumes almost 1,000 calories per day less than their counterpart in western Europe or the US. (In the South the average consumption is 2,500 calories daily while in western Europe it is 3,400 calories and in the United States it is 3,600 calories.)

This situation is by no means satisfactory and it is predicted that it will further deteriorate as the human population continues to grow. It would appear that, in the not too distant future, there will be a conflict between human beings' demand for food and the physical capacity of the earth to meet those needs. For example, between 1950 and 1984 the production of grain, the staple crop of millions of people, expanded at around 3 per cent per annum. This meant that it edged ahead of population growth and, thus, per capita consumption rose. Since 1984, however, despite improved technology, irrigation and petrochemicals, grain production has only expanded by 1 per cent per annum. This is a particularly troubling trend as population growth continues to rise, which means that per capita consumption is falling and will continue to do so.[3]

The range lands of the world which support flocks that provide humans with animal protein are also under stress. In the four decades between 1950 and 1990 beef and mutton production multiplied by 2.6 times. Once again this produced a 26 per cent per capita increase. However, because of the destruction of range lands, especially through overgrazing, beef and mutton production is not expected to continue rising even as the world's population increases.[4]

Poor land management, overgrazing, inappropriate agriculture, deforestation and population pressures have caused soil erosion, salinization and desertification on an unprecedented scale. The

United Nations Environment Programme has estimated that since 1945, 108 million acres of productive land has been lost to agriculture each year. This adds up to 4.85 billion acres or around 35 per cent of the earth's fertile land.[5] The UN estimates that of the world's 5,200 million hectares of agriculturally used dryland, 69 per cent is degraded or subjected to desertification. In Africa the figure runs as high as 73 per cent and in Asia 70 per cent. Because of the type of agriculture which is now being pursued worldwide, and the pressure to increase production to feed a world population that is growing by 90 million a year, it is almost inevitable that soil erosion will increase in the decades ahead. Sadly the loss of arable land through desertification and erosion is irreversible in historical time: it takes hundreds of years to create fertile topsoil.

THE LOSS OF BIODIVERSITY

Much of the tropical rainforests, which are one of the world's richest habitats, has already been destroyed with many ill-effects on agriculture, human livelihood, the health and productivity of rivers and estuaries, and local and global climate patterns. Perhaps the greatest tragedy is the huge extinction of species. No one knows how many species are on earth: estimates run between 5 million and 30 million species. Tens of thousands have already been destroyed. The Harvard biologist E. O. Wilson estimates that we are losing 10,000 species annually.[6]

Some people dismiss the whole question of extinction by claiming that it is a feature of the natural world. Whilst true, this view overlooks a number of important considerations. Firstly, the rate of extinction taking place today is between 1,000 and 10,000 times greater than the average rate during most of the past 65 million years. Secondly, major extinctions like those which took place at the end of the Permian and Cretaceous periods opened up possibilities for new life forms. They resembled a pruning of the biosphere and enhanced rather than destroyed diversity. Today, sadly, our industrial culture is sterilizing the planet and closing the door to future diversity.[7]

This also means destroying, for ever, potential sources of food to feed a larger human family. Despite the varied diets in different cultures around the world, humans currently use only 1 per cent of the known species as sources of nourishment. We use only 7,000 out of a potential 75,000 edible plants. Many species that we do not use today could easily become staple food sources, unless of course they are extinct.[8]

The scale of extinction is evident when one looks at what is happening to birds around the world. Human population increase has meant that land which was previously forested or open range land is now devoted to agricultural purposes. More important still, wetlands and estuaries, the traditional habitats for many bird species, have been colonized by humans. In the process they are often sprayed with chemicals like DDT, which are most injurious to birds, other animals and humans. A major collapse in the populations of birds of prey – peregrines, hawks and eagles – occurred in Europe and the US in the 1950s and 1960s. This was reversed somewhat in the 1970s after DDT was banned. DDT is still commonly used in many Southern countries, especially in the production of export-oriented crops, and it continues to cause serious damage to birds. According to a 1993 report by BirdLife International, a conservation group based in Cambridge, England, population levels among 70 per cent of the world's species are in decline and 1,000 species are threatened with outright extinction in the near future.[9]

Birds may not be the only creatures damaged by exposure to organochlorines. A 1991 multidisciplinary conference was held in the USA on the long-term health consequences for humans of organochlorines. Many of the speakers called attention to new, disturbing research on how these substances disrupt human physiology and cause cancer, infertility, suppression of the immune system, birth defects and stillbirths.[10]

Extinction is also an issue when fish stocks are considered. Worldwide, fish provide more than half the animal protein consumed by human beings. The proportion is even higher in many countries of the South. Unfortunately, fish supplies are not keeping pace with the increase in the human population. Between 1950 and 1989 fish catches, worldwide, rose dramatically from 20 to 100 million tons annually. But the ability of the seas to sustain that level of harvesting is not unlimited. According to the United Nations Food and Agriculture Organization (FAO), in 1993 nine out of the world's seventeen major fisheries were in serious decline and many stocks had already been devastated. The tonnage for 1992, despite improved ships and equipment, fell to 97 million.[11] The drop in catches from wild stock is even more dramatic: down from a historic peak of 82 million tons in 1989 to 77 million in 1991. Most analysts predict that the depletion of fish stocks will mean the harvest from the sea will continue to decline in the years ahead while world population levels will continue to rise.

The situation in the United States is typical of what is happening in many other countries. In the *New York Times* (7 March 1994), Timothy Egan wrote from Seattle that there had been a dramatic fall in the number of Pacific salmon and steelheads. Across the US in New Bedford, Massachusetts – a traditional fishing ground for the past 350 years – the Atlantic was 'largely barren of the great swarm of haddock, cod and flounder that sustained more than ten generations of New Englanders and became millions of fish sticks'. Overfishing and pollution were the main reasons for the decline.

A lead story in *Newsweek* (25 April 1994), entitled 'Empty nets: Too many fishermen, too few fish', confirmed that fish stocks around the world, from Canada to Chile to India, have been overfished. The depletion in some areas, like the North Sea, exceeds even that of the US: at present it is running at 65 per cent for many major stocks.

One can assume that humans have been fishing for tens of thousands of years without harming fish stocks. However, the damage today is being caused by the enormous impact of modern, high-tech fishing methods and huge factory ships. Large vessels, operated by a minimum of crew members, can travel to fishing grounds anywhere around the world, track shoals of fish on radar, electronically direct tent-like nets to capture the fish, and finally process them on board the ship. These operators can easily move from one productive fishing ground to the next.

The *Newsweek* article called for restraint and regulations to ensure that fish stocks are not permanently destroyed. The title, however, was misleading: there are not too many fishermen. In fact the authors admit that high-tech fishing endangers the livelihood of 38,000 fishermen each year in the Philippines. Their communities suffer from the loss of employment and shortage of fish protein in their daily diets. In normal circumstances local fishermen seldom overfish in their areas because their personal and community health is intimately bound up with fruitful seas. The real problem is the sophisticated technology, the large ships and the pressure on the owners and operators to return massive profits on their investments. Given those pressures, a sustainable yield from the oceans is impossible.

BREACHING LIMITS

The earth's resources are threatened with extinction not only through over-extraction but through over-exploitation and contamination. A 1991 study by Alexander King and Bertrand Schneider for the Council of the Club of Rome gave the same warning as the original report *Limits to Growth*.[12] The study focused not merely on the stress which continuous growth places on the resource side of the equation but also considered the unsustainable impact of continuous growth on the 'sink' side. This refers to the capacity of the biosphere to assimilate waste which has been created by humans. The authors say that these limits are being breached in a variety of crucial areas that need to be addressed urgently.

Ecological economics teaches that human economic activity must be understood as a subsystem within the larger ecosystems of the earth. Like plants and animals, humans need food and energy in order to sustain life. If the human species is to continue to reproduce and survive it must meet food and energy needs in a way that does not destroy the world. Humans must operate within the limits of the natural world, living, as it were, on the interest which nature provides without drawing down the ecological capital.

All plants obtain their energy from the Sun. Through the complex biochemistry of photosynthesis plants transform solar energy into usable energy in the form of sugars. This energy, in turn, becomes available for other creatures, the herbivores and carnivores. Plants are more efficient users of the Sun's energy – it takes vast quantities of plants to feed herbivores and still larger amounts in order to feed carnivores.

When the number and demands of a carnivorous species like humans increase dramatically this can put enormous pressure on other species within the biosphere. Scientists recognize that there is an upper limit to the amount of solar energy made available through the aggregate of the net primary product of photosynthesis. This encompasses all the solar energy made available to all creatures through the green matter of the earth. A study by Vitousek et al. (1986) estimated that humans have now captured 40 per cent of terrestrial energy for their own, exclusive use. If one includes the oceans the percentage drops to 25 per cent.[13] This finding is extremely important as it sets the context for the optimum scale of human activity, including economic activity, in relationship to the needs of creatures on earth. The call for a five- to tenfold increase in worldwide economic activity in *Our Common Future* (the Brundt-land Report written in 1987 for the World Commission on Environment and Development) appears totally unrealistic if Vitousek and his collaborators are right.

Another area where limits are being breached is in the use of fossil fuels. It is estimated that the level of carbon dioxide in the air has risen by 30 per cent since the beginning of the nineteenth century. This is mainly as a result of the increased burning of fossil fuels and the depletion of forests. This in turn may be leading to an increase in the earth's temperature through the greenhouse effect, where the sun's rays are trapped within the earth's own atmosphere. Some scientists predict that global warming could cause an average 2° to 3° Centigrade increase in surface air temperature. As a consequence the ice-caps will melt and sea levels will rise, inundating many low-lying areas. In this scenario many Pacific islands will simply disappear. River deltas in Egypt and Bangladesh and low-lying areas like Holland, home to tens of millions of people, will also be submerged and become uninhabitable. Although there is no absolute agreement among scientists that global warming is actually taking place, the evidence to date is compelling and is widely accepted by many scientists, especially, the UN Intergovernmental Panel on Climate Change (IPCC).

Other predicted changes include a significant drop in rainfall in many of the food-producing areas of the world, particularly in North America. This could have catastrophic consequences for global food production. The speed of the change will also accelerate species extinction. An increase in the ferocity and number of tropical storms is also predicted as a consequence of global warming. Many insurance companies claim that this is already happening. They point to the increase of such storms in the southern United States and the Pacific, and the resulting huge insurance claims. Hurricane Andrew in October 1992 cost around $20 billion. A report prepared for the world's largest insurance company, Munich Re, points to the link between global warming and more frequent hurricanes. Insurance companies, it seems, are among the few businesses in the corporate world which have begun to take global warming seriously.

Given these massive changes and consequent dislocation it would seem prudent to take decisive action now to prevent the runaway greenhouse effect. In May 1990 the IPCC called for a 60 per cent cut in current emissions of carbon dioxide and other greenhouse gases in order to stabilize their concentration in the atmosphere.

Unfortunately there is little political will in Northern countries to face this issue and to act decisively. Corporate interests, especially those in the coal and oil sectors, have lobbied very effectively to block any increase in taxes on fossil fuels. While scientists are painting appalling scenarios, politicians adopt a wait-and-see attitude. But the problem will not go away. In fact, if it is not faced, it will simply get worse.

THE NUCLEAR BURDEN

In recent years nuclear power has been presented as 'Green' energy – the perfect solution to the greenhouse problem. However, this is just the latest phase of the multi-million-pound PR campaign to promote nuclear power. In the early years of the industry the nuclear lobby argued that this power was safe, cheap and reliable. All these claims have been proved to be false. The expansion of nuclear power will create environmental, health, economic and security risks. Nuclear power is dangerous at every stage of the industry's operation, from the mining and milling of uranium to the disposal of nuclear waste.

Unfortunately, the volume of these poisonous wastes is increasing every year: by 1986 the eleven uranium mills in the United States alone had accumulated 191 million tonnes of tailings on the ground. There is a growing fear that radioactive and chemical poison from this material will seep into the groundwater and permanently contaminate it over a wide area. At Hanford, one of the main storage centres in the United States, 422,000 gallons of radioactive liquid waste leaked out of the storage tanks. Tritium has been detected in groundwater, strontium-90 has been found in the Columbia river and plutonium in the nearby soil.[14]

People working in nuclear power stations also face many health hazards. A report released in Bonn in 1987 by a committee composed of workers, trade union representatives and the proprietors of the nuclear industry recommended that certain types of cancers should be recognized as occupational diseases for workers in nuclear plants.[15]

The nuclear burden will continue to haunt humanity and the earth community for centuries as some of the elements are lethal for up to 250,000 years. Many people feel that it is a crime against future generations to develop nuclear power extensively and encourage its proliferation when no safe way has yet been found to store and dispose of nuclear waste. E. F. Schumacher, author of *Small Is Beautiful*, insisted that 'no place on earth can be shown to be safe for the disposing of nuclear waste'.[16]

The storage of nuclear waste is causing alarm in eastern and central Europe. There are six reactors at Kozloduy in northwest Bulgaria, close to the Danube. Inspectors from the International Atomic Energy Agency (IAEA) in Vienna found that the pools in which the radioactive spent fuel rods were being cooled were in a deplorable state. Before the collapse of the Soviet Union, spent fuel was shipped there for reprocessing and storage. Installations in Russia will now accept spent fuel only if the service is pre-paid in dollars. A dangerous stockpile is building up, housed in totally inadequate facilities. Ivan Uzunov, a physicist and adviser to the Bulgarian Parliament's Environmental Committee, reported that 'we now have 700 tons of spent fuel elements resting in swimming pools . . . If these ponds are breached because of an earthquake or some other accident, the spent fuel could melt down.' Uzunov continued 'It would cost us $1 billion to have the spent fuel reprocessed or stored in France, but we cannot afford it, we simply can't spare the foreign exchange'.[17]

If the present proliferation of nuclear power continues, a dramatic increase in nuclear leaks and accidents can be expected. Already serious accidents have taken place at Sellafield in Britain, Three Mile Island in the United States and, most notably, Chernobyl in the Ukraine. The Chernobyl accident caused 31 deaths immediately and an estimated 8,000 from the after-effects (though as can be seen below, that is a conservative figure).[18] Many more have suffered from acute radiation poisoning, while 135,000 had to be evacuated from the area. In 1993, a Ukranian government report estimated that approximately 650,000 people were directly affected.[19]

The explosion spewed out a cloud of radioactive material which spread across Europe, from Greece to Scandinavia and from the Ukraine to the west coast of Ireland. Were it not for the courage of men like Lt Col. Shuklin, the helicopter pilot who flew above Chernobyl directing those who poured cement on the stricken reactor, the fire would have spread to the other reactors, causing far worse damage locally and globally. Col. Shuklin is now suffering from radiation sickness. Most of the fire-fighters who worked at the site have since died from radiation sickness.

The environmental impact of Chernobyl is also long-lasting. Lakes and rivers in the area are contaminated. Fish have been caught with 400 times the concentration of caesium-200 found in similar fish elsewhere. Vegetation and livestock have also been affected. A 1991 Greenpeace report on the disaster asserted that 'vast areas have been contaminated and that the health of hundreds of thousands of people will have to be monitored continuously'. Vladimir Chernousenko, the scientific director in charge of the 30-kilometre exclusion zone around the plant, estimates that 'up to 10,000 lives have been lost . . . and, instead of focusing on the task of saving people, the system has set about suppressing all information about the disaster'.[20]

The spectre of another disaster is ever-present at Chernobyl and at numerous sites in central and eastern Europe. Of the 58 nuclear power stations operating in the area, 40 are of the older, Soviet-built design. There were serious flaws in the construction process, safety features are often disregarded (as they were at Chernobyl), and monitoring procedures are inadequate. The Swedish Prime Minister Carl Bildt has called for the closure of 40 of these plants. However, owing to the power of the nuclear and industrial lobby, the plants are still in operation despite the dangers.

The accident at Chernobyl was the result of faulty technology and human error. The potential for human error is a crucial factor in the whole nuclear debate. Should the human community commit itself irrevocably to a technology which is capable of such far-reaching and irreversible consequences? The more nuclear technology proliferates, the greater the possibility of similar accidents happening elsewhere, especially when the technology is exported to countries where there is insufficient scientific and technological knowledge and training available. One cannot also rule out the possibility that, given the widespread unrest in the modern world, terrorist groups may target nuclear installations or attempt to create their own crude weapons. Significant amounts of plutonium suitable for making nuclear weapons have been smuggled out of the former Soviet Union in recent years.[21]

Nuclear power is also more costly than power generated from conventional methods – oil or coal – and is much less versatile. In an *Ecologist* article, Jim Jeffery disputes the figures of the Central Electricity Generating Board (CEGB) in Britain, which claims that nuclear energy is cheaper than energy from fossil fuels. Jeffery maintains that electricity produced in coal–oil burning stations is significantly cheaper.[22] For many years in Britain the CEGB used misleading accounting methods to maintain that nuclear-generated electricity was cheaper than that generated from coal. Finally, in 1987, the Chairman of the CEGB admitted that nuclear power had not been cheaper after all. When one factors in the expense of decommissioning nuclear plants the costs rise astronomically. Most revealing of all, in July 1993 Sir John Bourn, the head of the National Audit Office in Britain, warned Members of Parliament that the total cost of decommissioning and reprocessing was 'a financial time bomb'. He estimated that the total cost could be as high as £40 billion.[23]

Limited energy resources raise serious questions about the direction of our present industrial society. Fossil fuels *are* limited in quantity, but so is uranium. Only by opting for fast-breeder reactors can uranium resources be stretched to meet even a percentage of the future projected needs of a continually expanding industrial society. However, choosing the stop-gap method of nuclear power means meeting our present energy needs in a way that puts at risk every succeeding generation of living organisms on planet Earth. And opting for this particular path puts a strain on other areas of society when it is facilitated by the use of public funds. A 1992 World Bank report estimated that while only 6 per cent of public research funds for energy is allocated to renewable sources of energy, 60 per cent is devoted to research into nuclear energy. Surely this needs to be changed.

Christians believe that the earth was created by God and is sustained by him. The Bible and Christian tradition affirm the goodness of creation and challenge human beings to be good stewards of creation. Because nuclear energy creates radioactive waste, for which there is no safe means of disposal, wise stewardship must surely preclude this option for Christians. Furthermore, it is irresponsible to create and operate a technology which has the potential for accidents like Chernobyl.

Those who believe in preserving the integrity of God's creation must join together to change direction before it is too late. During the fire at Chernobyl in 1986, Reactor 4 was covered in concrete. For the American journalist Don Hinrichsen this concrete 'sarcophagus' is a fitting symbol to the nuclear energy venture which is now dying. Popular opposition to nuclear power is now widespread in the US, Europe, Taiwan and other countries. The question is: will nuclear power in eastern Europe die quietly or go out with another bang?

CONSERVATION AND RENEWABLE ENERGY

In recent decades human beings have used energy in a totally profligate and unsustainable way. It is estimated that it takes planet Earth 10,000 years to create the energy that the worldwide economy consumes in a single day.[24] Once again the lion's share goes to Northern countries, which use over 80 per cent of the world's energy resources. Ernst U. von Weizsäcker of the Wuppertal Institute for Climate, Environment and Energy in Germany urges that the North must act first to reduce its energy consumption, as those economies are the main polluters and destroyers of the earth. Unfortunately the North is still being offered as a model for other countries to follow. Unless it becomes sustainable, the drive to copy Northern energy use in much of the rest of the world will only exacerbate environmental and social problems.[25]

Von Weizsäcker believes that the North should be able to cut back on the use of fossil fuels without too much dislocation for the majority of people. There are still enormous possibilities for energy-saving strategies. According to him, present technological and social innovations could yield a fourfold increase in energy productivity. Energy-saving domestic gas water heaters and gas and electric cookers can reduce energy use by half. Well-insulated houses can reduce domestic heating consumption by almost 90 per cent. There is a potential for reducing energy use in electronic equipment by four-fifths. The technologies to achieve most of these transformations are already available, yet they are not being used because many corporations have profited handsomely from our present wasteful energy use. It is believed, for example, that a car which can deliver 100 miles to the gallon has been kept under wraps. It goes without saying that investment in public transport is even more important than producing fuel-efficient cars.

The present wasteful use of energy and raw materials is directly related to the low price of fossil fuels obtained since World War II. Cheap energy supports the illusion that it makes good economic sense to waste non-renewable sources of energy. To change this perception von Weizsäcker argues that 'Green taxes' should be introduced to reflect the real cost of oil production. Such costs should cover extraction, distribution and the expenses entailed in dealing with the negative impact of fossil fuels on the environment and human health. The tax should also stimulate energy and resource-use efficiency. One can expect that by penalizing the wasteful and pollutive use of energy and resources, businesses will be encouraged to invest in new, innovative, clean energy sources.

Some people may groan at the thought of another tax on the shoulders of people who feel over-taxed. For this reason many proponents of 'Green taxes' recommend that they should be revenue-neutral. This means that the revenue collected on polluting forms of energy and throw-away products ought to make it possible for governments to reduce substantially the burden of income and sales taxes. It would simply mean shifting taxes away from income and labour, which often leads to unemployment, to energy use and dirty industries. Then it would make good economic sense to conserve energy and curtail and phase out polluting industries.

Since gainful and good work is important, especially at a time of large-scale unemployment, it is important to point out that an energy tax would lead to more employment. The Council on Economic Priorities in the US reported that investment in energy-efficient technologies produced four times more jobs than would be provided by building new power stations.[26]

The impact of a 'Green' energy tax would also be felt in agriculture. Cheap fossil fuel favours large agribusinesses which enjoy economies of scale. This gives them a distinct price advantage over small family farms which produce food in a conserving and organic way. Within the present economic climate the reasons are simple. Big companies have easy access to cheap credit, heavy machinery, chemical pesticides, fertilizers, automated processing units and nationwide outlets. However, while the food they produce might be cheap, the environmental, human and animal welfare costs are very high. These include the loss of topsoil, increased toxicity of the soil, depleted aquifers, the loss of biodiversity, appalling conditions for animals, poor-quality food (often with toxic residues), rural decline and depopulation.

A substantial tax on energy could help turn all that around and support family farming and local food production. More expensive energy would favour smaller farming units, organic methods of food production and more employment in agriculture. This, in turn, would mean fresh, nutritious food, less processing and transport costs, better care of the land and livestock, sustainable production, greater diversity of products, and more viable, creative human communities.

An energy tax would achieve a number of desirable goals. Firstly, it would remove the hidden subsidy which favours agribusinesses and undermines family farming. Secondly, like any good tax it would penalize harmful behaviour, in this case the destructive farming methods of corporate agriculture, while at the same time stimulating good, sustainable and humane farming practices. In the light of the challenges which the human community faces in many parts of the world in the area of food production, such a tax is long overdue.

Von Weizsäcker recommends that this tax be introduced gradually to avoid disruption. This would allow sufficient time for increased investment in innovative technology, new infrastructures and, more important, promote major cultural changes which will be essential in order to establish a sustainable economy. A 5 per cent annual increase in price for energy derived from fossil fuels or nuclear power would gradually shift the balance in energy costs away from the wasteful use of fossil fuels towards more efficient uses and more benign sources of energy such as solar, wind, small-scale hydroelectricity, wave energy and biomass.

There is a huge potential for growth in the production of alternative sources of energy. It is estimated that one-tenth of the European Union's electricity needs could be met from wind power within 40 years. The British Wind Energy Association claims that research by the Department of the Environment shows that land-based wind farms could at present supply one-sixth of the United Kingdom's electricity needs, and that figure would jump to 50 per cent if off-shore sites were used.[27] Studies have shown that 'despite a recent spate of adverse publicity, electricity-generating wind farms are popular with people who live nearby'.[28] There is great potential also for wave energy. It is estimated that it could meet three-quarters of the EU's current energy needs if it was fully developed. In short, the potential for energy-saving and renewable energy sources is great. Even the US Environmental Protection Agency (EPA) believes that within 20 years one-third of the world's energy needs could be met by renewable sources of energy, as against one-seventh in 1990.

One reason why this potential has not been pursued to date is that the corporations which control the fossil fuel and nuclear industries have promoted the myth that clean sources of energy cannot supply the energy needs of the modern world. This, however, is untrue. Many renewable forms of energy are now almost on a par with fossil fuels and are less expensive than nuclear power, especially when all the costs are added up. There is a pressing need for much greater resources to be made available to research and promote these non-polluting forms of energy. Only in this way will they become cheaper and more readily available. Much more public money is still spent on research into nuclear power than on research into alternative, 'soft energy' paths. Greenpeace estimates that only 1 per cent of the World Bank's funding for energy projects is devoted to energy-saving projects.

Since global warming will affect every area of the globe the North must be willing to provide the financial resources and technical assistance to help transfer energy-saving and clean technologies to Southern countries. In this way Southern countries will be able to avoid the pitfalls which have befallen Northern countries through their addiction to fossil fuels. With less greenhouse gases being emitted into the atmosphere everyone will gain from this sharing.

LIMITED INDUSTRIAL ACTIVITY AND WASTE

Renewable energy and clean technology will play their part in the attempt to limit global damage, but industrial and consumer activity threaten global health in other ways. Chemicals and gases produced by industrial activity, especially CFCs, are interfering with the way ozone is created and broken down, threatening to reduce its concentration in the upper atmosphere. In recent years a hole the size of the United States has appeared over Antarctica each spring. For the past three years a similar, though smaller, hole has also been detected over the northern hemisphere.

Ozone filters out much of the Sun's ultraviolet radiation. Cancer specialist Dr John Healy reckons that for every 1 per cent reduction in ozone protection there is a corresponding 3 to 5 per cent increase in skin cancers and a 0.5 per cent increase in melanomas.[29] Increased ultraviolet radiation also damages the immune system and causes widespread crop losses. Alan Wellburn, Professor of Biochemistry at Lancaster University in Britain, estimates that ozone depletion could cause a 10 per cent loss of barley, peas and beans. He believes that the farming community is 'totally unprepared for this'.[30]

Data on ozone depletion do not often appear on the front pages of the newspaper or on the TV news, and yet it is extremely serious. Dr Joe Waters, who monitors ozone depletion for the National Aeronautics and Space Administration (NASA), is clearly worried by what is happening. He is quoted in the *Guardian* (14 February 1992) as saying 'people have just got to realize that we are talking about a threat to life on earth'.

The unsustainability and vulnerability of our present industrial and commercial society is also very evident when one looks at it from the other end – the ever-increasing mound of waste which is created by our throw-away culture. Many of the items manufactured by our industrial society are not necessary for human well-being and end up in rubbish dumps. *Newsweek* (27 November 1989) portrayed the industrial world being 'buried alive' in waste. The statistics are astounding: each consumer in the industrial world accumulates 3.5 pounds of rubbish every day.

Where to put this rubbish is becoming a major problem. It is now cluttering up landfills in towns and cities around the world. Many communities are simply running out of space. The US, with its affluence and disposable mentality, is by far the worst offender. Each year Americans throw away 16 billion disposable diapers, 1.6 billion pens, 2 billion razors and razor blades, and 220 million tyres. They discard enough aluminium to rebuild the entire US commercial airline fleet every three months. But space to dump things in is running out. In the US 80 per cent of solid waste is dumped into landfills. But their number is now shrinking. In the past ten years almost 5,000 have been filled and shut down. More than two-thirds of the landfills in the US have been closed since the late 1970s.

In former West Germany 35,000 of the 50,000 landfill sites have been declared potentially dangerous because they threaten vital groundwater supplies which could contaminate drinking water and water used for agriculture. The disposal of toxic waste is particularly worrying. The chemical and pharmaceutical industries often claim that they are very responsible and know what they are doing. This, unfortunately, is not always the case. Of the 48,000 chemicals listed by the EPA in the US, very little is known about the toxic effects of 38,000. Fewer than 1,000 have been tested for acute effects and only about 500 for cancer-causing, reproductive or mutagenic effects. This is not very reassuring.

In Paul Hawken's view the concept of a toxic waste dump is similar to that of a prison. Humans round up 'dangerous chemicals' and lock them up together on a single site. Unlike human gaols, where inmates spend a few years or at the most a few decades, toxic waste 'gaols' will need to be guarded for hundreds or even thousands of years. It is not very reassuring to be told that 'at present there is no known means to completely detoxify and render harmless most of these substances. We have no idea how to place or recycle them back into the environment in such a way that they become harmless and safe.'[31]

Not surprisingly the growth in the not-in-my-back-yard (NIMBY) mentality means that communities would like to move the rubbish elsewhere. Trains and trucks loaded with garbage criss-cross the US. First World people wish to keep their own nests clean; so the Two-Thirds World is often seen as a soft option for dumping toxic waste. *Time* (2 January 1989) carried an account of the voyage of the *Pelicano*. For two years it sailed around the world seeking a port that would accept its 14,000-ton cargo of toxic ash. In October 1989 the *Pelicano* illegally dumped 4,000 pounds of its cargo off Haiti and may have dumped the rest overboard on the high seas. The *Pelicano* is a clear symbol of the final twist in the saga of the First World's exploitation of the Third World. Having for centuries abused their resources and human labour, the First World is now completing the circle of exploitation by dumping its toxic waste on unsuspecting Third World people.

Within the remit of conventional economics it seems sensible for powerful Northern nations, whose citizens place a high premium on a clean environment, to export waste to poor, Southern nations. There was a furore in 1991 when Dr Lawrence Summers, then chief economist of the World Bank, argued that 'the economic logic of dumping a load of toxic waste in the lowest-wage country is impeccable'.[32] Of course, many Third World leaders were incensed. The industrialized world generates over 90 per cent of the estimated 237 to 273 million tons of hazardous waste produced worldwide each year. It is estimated that it costs between £200 and £1,000 to dispose of one ton of toxic waste in Europe, therefore the attraction of dumping it cheaply in the Third World is irresistible.

In the 1980s much of the waste was dumped in Africa. After some well-publicized incidents in Nigeria the Organization of African Unity (OAU) called for a ban on waste imports in 1988. This was formalized in 1991 when the Bamako Convention was signed. In 1993 the countries of Central America followed suit. As more and more countries prohibit the importation of toxic waste the waste traders are turning to South-east and South Asia as a final destination. Plastic waste exports to South Asia have increased dramatically in the past two years. In January 1993, 53 per cent of total US plastic waste exports were sent to Bangladesh, India and Pakistan. Pepsi Cola alone, it was alleged, shipped over 7,000 tons of plastic scraps to India. In response to enquiries from Greenpeace investigators, Pepsi denied that it exports any scraps to India.[33] Waste merchants from Britain, Germany, Australia and Canada also shipped an increased tonnage of toxic waste to these poor countries.

Thankfully the situation is set to improve. Greenpeace International hailed the Basel Convention in March 1994 as a striking environmental victory. This bans the export of toxic waste from rich Northern countries to poor Southern countries from the end of 1997. Predictably, the countries which have gained most from exporting waste – Australia, Canada, Finland, Germany, Japan, the United Kingdom and the United States – opposed the ban. Greenpeace's lobbying of the Group of 77 and the decision of EU Environment Ministers to support the ban turned the tide in favour of ratifying the Convention. Pope John Paul II also threw his weight behind the ban. Speaking in Rome on 22 October 1993, he said:

> It is a grave abuse and an offence against the solidarity of humanity when industrial enterprises of rich countries profit from the weak economies and legislation of poorer countries by exporting dirty technologies and waste which degrade the environment and health of the population.[34]

One option that is often proposed as a dream solution to waste is incineration. The unsightly rubbish simply goes up in smoke. Promoters of waste burning claim it is a safe method of waste management. In reality, incineration releases toxins into the air, land and water. A study in New Jersey of the state-of-the-art incinerator with a 2,250-ton daily capacity found that in the course of one year it will emit 5 tons of lead, 17 tons of mercury, 580 pounds of cadmium, 2,248 tons of nitrous oxide, 853 tons of sulphur, 777 tons of hydrogen chloride, and 87 tons of sulphuric acid.[35]

As if that poisonous cocktail were not enough, incineration creates dioxins and furans, both generally believed to be cancer-causing. Incineration does not destroy matter, it simply changes the chemical composition and toxicity of the matter which is burned. The incinerator acts as a chemical synthesizer. It burns rubbish at very high temperatures, ranging from 400° to 1,600° Centigrade, and in the process complex organic molecules are broken down into basic atoms. However, when the combustion gas cools on its way up the chimney some of the atoms recombine to create other compounds. These products of incomplete combustion (PICs) can be even more toxic than the original material which was burned. For example, the lignin from paper and wood combines with chlorine gases to form 210 different dioxin compounds. Most are highly toxic and cancer-causing. Dioxins have been produced by every municipal solid-waste incinerator ever tested. They are also produced in all hazardous-waste incinerators.

For years controversy surrounded the connection between dioxins and cancer. In 1976 dioxins were released into the atmosphere after an accident at a chemical plant in Italy. Though a large area was contaminated few people seemed to develop cancer. This raised questions about the link between dioxins and cancer. A new study published in 1993 in the journal *Epidemiology* told a different story. It showed that people who were exposed to dioxins are now exhibiting excessive cancers.[36] Even the US's EPA has reappraised its position on dioxins and now holds that 'dioxin does cause cancer in humans'.

Incineration is not a magic process. The residue of toxic fly ash, which amounts to approximately 30 tons for every 100 tons of rubbish, has to be disposed of in dumps lined with a special kind of plastic. Some of the toxins are dangerous for hundreds of years, yet the plastic lining in the dumps is only guaranteed for twenty years. Problems may arise even before that: some landfills have reported leaks within months of construction. These toxins can cause cancer, birth defects, miscarriages and foetal toxicity. They can also damage the reproductive system, cause sterility, weaken the immune system, and cause liver and kidney damage. The clean image cultivated by the promoters of incineration is sullied by such revelations.

Proponents of incineration, which normally include industry and government agencies, often portray it as a feasible, safe and cheap technology. Incineration provides a way for industry and public authorities to avoid confronting the waste issue. It also saves them from investing in clean technology. For them it is the convenient, profitable and liability-free way to mask today's problems and pass them on to future generations. However, when all the costs are counted incineration is expensive. In the US, in 1986, the real cost to industry to incinerate 1 ton of waste was $100 per ton. If the top 50 producers had to pay the full price it would have cost them $20 billion, or more than eight times their profits. In fact, these corporations did not pay these rates because both the construction and running of the incinerators was subsidized by taxpayers' money.[37]

The theme of this chapter is that industrial culture is sterilizing the earth and, in the final analysis, it is unsustainable. Unlimited economic growth, which is assumed in much of the contemporary business and economic literature, is simply impossible on a finite planet. The environmental movement is constantly trying to highlight the importance of developing ways of living which do not destroy ecological capital, yet this perspective is not universally shared.

NICS: NOT THE BEST MODELS

The spectacular economic growth which a number of countries in Asia have achieved in recent years seems to invalidate the above analysis. These newly industrialized countries (NICs) were desperately poor until recent decades. However, in the space of a few short years they have experienced remarkable prosperity. The NICs, often called 'tiger' economies, normally include South Korea, Taiwan, Singapore, Hong Kong and, more recently, Malaysia, Thailand and southern China. These countries have been held up as models for other 'developing' countries by international institutions like the World Bank and the IMF, and by economists like Milton Friedman.[38] (Their record on human rights and the social and environmental costs of rapid industrialization are passed over, however.) It is worth noting that these countries are not paragons of virtue, however, as far as 'free trade' is concerned: in each case the State has taken an interventionist approach, especially in the areas of promoting trade and making cheap credit available.

For the past two decades orthodox development policy-makers at both the IMF and the World Bank have been encouraging the next wave of poor countries to follow the NICs' lead. The theory is that when this group, in turn, have made it up the ladder of economic development, another wave of poor countries can emulate them, and so on until the whole world reaches the top rung of development.

The underlying development theory predicted that the first group of NICs would move out of textiles and light electronic manufacturing as soon as they moved up a stage on the ladder of industrial processing. This has not happened. They simply have widened their range of activities to include both light and heavy industry, and simple and complex processes.

Another factor which will severely limit the possibility of other countries emulating the NICs is that the microchip revolution of the late 1970s has now made it possible for TNCs to fragment their production processes in a way that was not possible in the early stages of this industrial revolution. The original NICs developed integrated industries like steel, car manufacturing and shipbuilding. The potential for 'value-added' gains and spin-off benefits for industry and services was enormous. Today the 'value-added' gains for would-be NICs are very modest when the cost of imported raw materials is included. In the present phase most of the financial benefits are siphoned off elsewhere.

Rivalry between NICs has also put pressure on them to lower labour costs and commodity prices further in order to capture a larger share of foreign investment. Some economists at the World Bank were aware that such economic policies pit one country against another. Hollis Chenery and Donald Keesing forecast that 'the increasing number of successful competitors may make it increasingly difficult for newcomers to get established' and that the success of 'a few' could leave 'too little' opportunity for the rest.[39] Furthermore, the increased number of NICs chasing dwindling markets in the First World also depresses the prices of finished goods and trims profit margins.

Finally, the initial leap in the tiger economies was achieved at the expense of workers and the environment. Walden Bello and Stephanie Rosenfeld in *Dragons in Distress* point out that 'high-speed growth without environmental controls has converted Taiwan into a poisoned paradise of free-wheeling capitalists, leading increasing numbers of Taiwanese to a willingness to trade rapid growth for ecological equilibrium'.[40] Much the same message is contained in *Taiwan 2000*, the comprehensive study of the impact of rapid industrialization on the Taiwanese environment (which I referred to in Chapter 2).[41] That report acknowledges that:

> Taiwan today is experiencing the consequences of 30 years of commitment to economic growth at any cost. Production has grown at rates that are the envy of the world, and consumption has followed closely. The environment has been left almost unprotected to absorb the by-products of production and consumption. Serious problems have developed; accumulation of solid and hazardous wastes, air and water pollution, and destabilized natural resource systems. (p. iv)

The comments on the disposal of hazardous waste are frightening. It states that 'with few, if any, disposal facilities and no institutional mechanisms to ensure the safe disposal of such substances it is suspected that large quantities of hazardous wastes have been dumped into rivers or onto the ground, or, at best, into rusting barrels' (p. iv). In many regions groundwater is polluted and 'there is a clear basis to expect this to worsen in the future' (p. 22).

The report is adamant that remedial action needs to be taken now and that this demands integrated policies and programmes. It states that 'the situation will not take care of itself. If environmental protection is not given high priority in the national policy agenda and forces now in operation are allowed to continue unabated, the entire island of Taiwan will be in danger of becoming a poisonous garbage dump' (p. 11).

Taiwan 2000 ends by repeating a well-known Chinese cautionary folktale. The story describes the behaviour of a poor family which, through good luck and hard work, had become rich. Once they had 'made it' they neglected their land, stopped repairing the irrigation canals and became contemptuous of the difficult work of maintaining soil fertility. At the same time they spent money foolishly and fell into debt. In a short period of time their wealth disappeared and they were reduced, once again, to poverty. *Taiwan 2000* insists that:

> Taiwan's present situation has some very disturbing analogies to this story . . . Thrift, hard work and cleverness have given us a standard of living that is higher than anything enjoyed in any previous period of history. Long life is the norm . . . food is so varied and abundant that we are more afraid of getting fat than of facing a famine. Modern technology provides service, comforts, conveniences, entertainments, and improvements . . . Yet, if we continue along the present path, by the year 2000 we can expect to be in a precarious position, and to find much of the good things we now enjoy have had hidden costs . . . We have frequently overlooked management of the physical and biological resources that support us, and have accepted debts to the future by pursuing present and personal gain without consideration of long-term costs and sustainability . . . We have gotten into the habit of doing almost nothing to repair the damage our activities cause to nature, or to clean up the garbage and poisonous by-products that result from our frantic rates of activity. (p. 40)

Even after the publication of *Taiwan 2000* (in 1989) little action has been taken by the government. The former head of the Taiwanese Environmental Protection Agency Jaw Shau-Kong complained in 1992 that 'where environment protection clashed with economic development, the environment is usually sacrificed'.[42] The *China Morning Post*, in the same editorial, complained that 'Taiwan's environment is so badly damaged that only drastic, aggressive efforts can save it'.

The cost involved in South Korea's industrialization drive is equally high. Jang Won, Professor at the Department of Environmental Engineering at Tae-Jon University, reports that the annual mean level of sulphur dioxide and nitrogen dioxide concentrations in Seoul are among the highest in the world. Hospitals have reported increasing numbers of patients with bronchitis, asthma and pneumonia. The worst pollution is in the huge industrial export zones. Many of the substances which are regularly released into the environment – like benzene, asbestos, vinyl chloride, mercury and cadmium – are cancer-producing substances. Acid rain is also taking its toll on lakes and trees.

Workers in many plants are routinely exposed to toxic substances. Numerous workers at the Wonjin rayon factory in Kurin City have died from a debilitating illness caused by exposure to carbon disulphide (CS_2) poisoning. CS_2 is an organic solvent used in making rayon, which is a lining material for coats and suits. Until recently, conditions at the plant were primitive. Workers were not issued with face masks which might provide some protection against the gas. According to Dr Gil-Seong Yang, who has treated many of the victims, scores of workers have died while others have been incapacitated for life. Only recently, after street protests, has the government (which owns the company) accepted any responsibility for what has happened and agreed to pay compensation. The figures are low: the usual amount offered to a worker who is already crippled and, possibly, facing death is a mere $14,000. According to Professor Park Hyun Seo of Hanyang University in Seoul, who has campaigned on behalf of the workers, successive South Korean governments were so intent on industrializing the economy that economic expansion took precedence over everything, including the lives of the workers.

Water pollution is also widespread and this has adversely affected human health and the fishing industry in many coastal areas. *Activity News* said that large companies such as Hyundai, Doosan, Samsung and Lucky-Goldstar are among the leading polluters. In March and April 1991, for example, several hundred tons of phenol was leaked into the Naktong river by the Doosan group.[43] Even municipal water supplies are contaminated by sewage and industrial waste. A report by the Construction Ministry, carried out in August

1989, found that almost all tap water was polluted. This shocked the country but the government immediately moved to criticize the study and assure people that the water was safe.

South Korea's growing environmental havoc is a direct result of three decades of export-oriented growth, where the government turned a blind eye to pollution. Until recently environmental legislation was weak and full of loopholes. Monitoring agencies were not equipped to carry out their tasks effectively and their procedures were often secret. Even when polluters are prosecuted many do not pay their fines. In 1989, 90 per cent of fines went unpaid. Despite the destruction of the air, water and soil of the country, and the consequent health hazards posed by such pollution, the maximum gaol sentence for offenders is only five years. This is hardly surprising, since very few people in Northern countries, either, have gone to prison for environmental offences.

The high economic growth rates in Taiwan, South Korea and other tiger economies, which have lifted millions out of poverty, have come at the huge price of extensive and irreversible environmental destruction. Industrial pollution, toxic waste, deforestation, soil erosion, polluted groundwater and the loss of natural habitats will ensure that the development is not sustainable. The so-called developing countries, instead of attempting to emulate South Korea and Taiwan in the arena of an increasingly hostile and turbulent world economic climate, would be much better off gearing their economies to meeting the needs of their own people.

NO LIMITS?

In spite of all the evidence and gloomy predictions some commentators fail to recognize the notion of limits and continue to promote the current damaging economic and industrial policies. In September 1993 *The Economist* invited a number of well-known figures to attempt to forecast how things might look during the next 150 years.[44] Over twenty authors reflected on a host of issues including the future of democracy, education, technology, morality and appropriate economic systems. Though there were some differences of emphasis, most of the authors were optimistic about the future. They expected that free trade and the market economy would continue to dominate the next 150 years and go from strength to strength. Most claimed that the market economy had brought unimaginable prosperity and affluence to the 'developed' Western nations since World War II. Given such success at boosting economic growth, many contributors exhorted former socialist countries, and what they termed the 'developing' world, to embark on this same journey if they wished to achieve prosperity.

One contributor, C. Fred Bergsten, felt that the future for capitalism is rosy. The challenge, as he saw it, is 'to stimulate economic efficiency, growth and equitable income distribution' (p. 53). The concepts of what might be an appropriate scale for human activities or a preference for bioregionalism were absent. In fact, those who oppose large conglomerates and believe that 'small is beautiful' are ridiculed as 'playing King Canute to the rising tides of the benefits of globalism' (p. 54). Nowhere was the connection between the cheap availability of fossil fuels and the rise of modern industrialization adequately discussed.

In the same issue, the deputy editor Clive Crook wrote of the 'triumph of capitalism' in recent years 'in the collapse of communism and the spread of the market economics to the Third World' (p. 48). He praised the achievements of capitalism: 'No other economic system even comes close to matching its achievements in any aspect of economic or social progress' (p. 48). In an attempt to calm fears that capitalism might be in retreat, because economic growth rates have slipped to 2 per cent per annum in recent years, Crook reminded readers that 2 per cent growth is enough to double output in a mere 35 years. He did not refer to the fact that the present level of global output is taxing the resource, energy and sink capacities of the biosphere. A doubling of this within a short period of time would surely be catastrophic.

Crook's presentation points to the crucial need for a new, more accurate vocabulary with which to address, in an adequate way, many of the issues facing our modern world. It is difficult to enter into serious discussion with people when the language used is so misleading. The word 'development', used in this context, has a positive semantic connotation. However, viewed from an ecological perspective 'development' has involved widespread and often irreversible damage to the earth.

There was very little questioning among the contributors about how a growing population and rising standards of living for 5 to 10 billion people could be accommodated within the limits of the biosphere. Very few mentioned the limitations which a finite world places on human acquisitiveness. Even those who did, like the Governor of Hong Kong Chris Patten, felt that there was no conflict between promoting free trade and displaying a concern for the environment. Interestingly enough, Patten felt that 'environmental policy [ought to become] a larger part of international diplomacy' rather than an integral dimension of economics. The environment figured briefly in Michael Walzer's long article on future political configurations. He conceded that 'quality [of life] is not a matter of meaningfulness or authenticity . . . [but] is closer to a matter of survival' (p. 47). If survival *is* the issue, it received very little attention.

Diane Ravitch, a historian of education and visiting Fellow at the Brookings Institution in Washington DC, claimed that 'education will be shaped by . . . changes in demography, technology and the family' (p. 39). The content of education will remain much the same: 'languages, science, history, government, economics, geography, mathematics and arts, as well as the skills necessary to understand today's problems and its technologies'. She was more interested in the challenges to education posed by multi-culturalism and new technologies than in the challenge which the ecological crisis poses. Teaching students the story of the universe, and the role of individuals and different communities within this story, did not figure in her view of education.

As the notion of limits impinges more on the collective human consciousness it will become obvious that the affluence of the First World cannot be replicated by every country in the world. The range of data presented here reveals where humans are breaching the capacity of the earth to renew itself and absorb our pollution. Current human industrial activity is changing the chemistry of the air and water, altering the hydrological cycle and upsetting the entire self-renewing pattern of nature which has taken millions of years to emerge. We are causing changes of a biological and geological order of magnitude and are only now beginning to wake up to the consequences of our activity. There is a deep irony in the whole saga. In recent centuries we have set out, through the mediation of science and technology, to make nature subservient to human decisions and in the process make human beings as independent as possible of nature. While the endeavour has provided enormous comforts for a small segment of humanity, it has impoverished the vast majority of people and is now threatening the very survival of many of the earth's most important ecosystems and natural cycles.

NOTES
1   Tim Lang and Colin Hines, *The New Protectionism: Protecting the Future Against Free Trade* (London: Earthscan Publications, 1993), pp. 75–6.

2   Thomas Pakenham, *The Scramble for Africa* (London: Abacus, 1991).
3   Lester R. Brown, 'A decade of discontinuity', *World Watch* (July/August 1993), pp. 19–23.
4   Lester Brown, *The State of the World* (Washington DC: Worldwatch Institute, 1994), p. 179.
5   Paul Hawken, *The Ecology of Commerce: A Declaration of Sustainability* (New York: HarperCollins, 1993), pp. 22–3.
6   E. O. Wilson, *Biophilia* (Cambridge, MA: Harvard University Press, 1984), p. 122.
7   Paul Hawken, op. cit., p. 29.
8   Ibid.
9   Howard Young, 'Flying into trouble', *World Watch* (January/February 1994), pp. 10–19.
10 Paul Hawken, op. cit., p. 41.
11 Ibid., p. 23.
12 Alexander King and Bertrand Schneider, *The First Global Revolution: A Report by the Council of the Club of Rome* (London: Simon and Schuster, 1991).
13 P. M. Vitousek, P. R. Ehrlich, A. H. Ehrlich and P. A. Matson, 'Human appropriation of the products of photosynthesis', *Bioscience*, vol. 34, no. 6 (1986), pp. 368–73.
14 Edward Goldsmith and Nicholas Hildyard (eds), *The Earth Report* (London: Mitchell Beazley, 1988), p. 188.
15 *Philippine Daily Inquirer* (30 April 1987).
16 E. F. Schumacher, *Small Is Beautiful* (London: Harper & Row, 1973), p. 136.
17 Quoted in Don Hinrichsen, 'Russian roulette', *The Ashling Magazine* (Aran Islands; August 1993), pp. 68–71.
18 Julian Borger, 'Forgotten few who live in the shadow of Chernobyl', *Guardian* (22 April 1994), p. 9.
19 Uinsionn MacDubhghaill, 'Health risks linger near Chernobyl', *Irish Times* (5 November 1993).
20 Dick Hogan, 'The children of Chernobyl', *Irish Times* (5 July 1991).
21 Patricia Clough, 'Alarm at nuclear smuggling', *Sunday Times* (14 August 1994).
22 J. W. Jeffrey, 'The collapse of nuclear economics', *The Ecologist* (January/February 1988), pp. 9–14.
23 'Nuclear shut-down is financial time bomb, Audit chief tells MPs', *Guardian* (1 July 1993).
24 Paul Hawken, op. cit., pp. 21–2.
25 Ernst U. von Weizsäcker, 'Why the North must act first' in *Sustainable Growth* (Geneva: Visser 't Hooft Endowment Fund for Leadership Development (5 route des Morillons, 1218 Grand-Saconnex), 1993).
26 Paul Hawken, op. cit., p. 183.
27 Martyn Halsall, 'Energy alternative blowing in the wind', *Guardian* (29 January 1991).
28 Crispin Aubrey, 'Shelter from the storm', *Guardian* (8 April 1994). A 1994 study shows that between 74 and 83 per cent of people living near three Welsh wind farms find them acceptable developments. Similar findings come from the Lake District and West Sussex.
29 Dex Nix, 'Ozone fears of skin cancer increase here', *Sunday Press* (Dublin: 15 March 1992).
30 Sean Ryan, 'Race to clean up the atmosphere as ozone hole drifts southwards', *Sunday Times* (1 March 1992).
31 Paul Hawken, op. cit., p. 46.
32 Quoted in Jim Pucket, 'Disposing of the waste trade', *The Ecologist* (March/April 1994).
33 Ann Leonard, 'South Asia, the new target of international waste traders', *Multinational Monitor* (December 1993), pp. 21–4.

34   Quoted in a Greenpeace brochure, *Opportunity at Basel* (March 1994).
35   Paul Hawken, op. cit., pp. 46–7.
36   Peter Montague, 'Dioxin causes cancer, says US environmental agency', *Third World Resurgence*, no. 39 (November 1993), pp. 9–10.
37   Paul Hawken, op. cit., p. 47.
38   Milton Friedman, 'The second Industrial Revolution', *Far Eastern Economic Review* (28 October 1993), p. 23.
39   Quoted in Robin Broad and John Cavanagh, 'No more NICs', *Foreign Policy* (Fall 1988), p. 83.
40   Walden Bello and Stephanie Rosenfeld, *Dragons in Distress: Asia's Miracle Economies in Crisis* (San Francisco: Food First/Institute for Food and Development Policy, 1990), p. 3.
41   *Taiwan 2000* (Nanking, Taipei: Institute of Ethnology, Academia Sinica, 1989).
42   'Environment needs more attention', *China Morning Post* (22 November 1992).
43   'It's already late', *Activity News*, newsletter of the National Council of Churches in Korea (October-December 1991).
44   'The next 150 years', *The Economist* (11–17 September 1993).

CHAPTER 4

World finance, local debt, global destruction

BOTH THE WORLD BANK and the International Monetary Fund (IMF) have subscribed to the neo-classical view of economic development. This involves promoting economic growth, free trade, untrammelled entry of foreign investment, and the integration of local economies into the global economy. Until recently the Bank gave little thought to the fact that its policies, which it has invested with an aura of immutability, might actually be impoverishing people and destroying, irreversibly, essential ecosystems like the rainforests. This chapter will expose the policies of the World Bank and the IMF and put the case for reform of such institutions.

THE WORLD BANK: SERVING WHOSE INTEREST?

The 'World' Bank is composed of a number of financial institutions – the International Bank for Reconstruction and Development (IBRD) and its affiliated institutions, the International Finance Corporation (IFC), and the International Development Agency (IDA). The IBRD and the IMF emerged in the aftermath of the International Monetary and Financial Conference which was held at Bretton Woods, New Hampshire in July 1944. The IBRD finances its lending operations mainly by borrowing on the capital markets of the world. It charges its borrowers what the Bank calls 'a market rate of interest'. This includes both the cost of the capital to the Bank and a margin for expenses. The IDA was established in 1960 to do more or less what the IBRD does but it specializes in lending at concessional terms (low or interest-free rates) to Third World countries whose GNP falls below an agreed poverty level. It draws its resources mainly from wealthier countries.

The World Bank promotes itself as an institution battling to eliminate poverty in the South. Critics of the Bank, most recently Bruce Rich in *Mortgaging the Earth*, tell another story. For three decades they have highlighted the poor environmental and development record of the World Bank and the IMF. They also insist that autocratic, secretive and non-participative procedures are faulty instruments with which to promote people-centred sustainable development.[1] In 1994 politicians have also added their voices to this chorus of criticism. A speech by the US Treasury Secretary Lloyd Bentsen at a World Bank spring meeting in 1994 contained a withering criticism of the Bank. Echoing the NGO demand for greater participation, Mr Bentsen told the 24 Finance Ministers who had assembled for the meeting that 'we have put too much emphasis on the top-down approaches that do not work. Experience shows the importance of ensuring the early and meaningful involvement of local people and non-government organizations.'[2]

Although the Articles of Agreement prohibit the World Bank and its officers from interfering 'in the political affairs of any member', it is, in fact, a very powerful political institution. It has enormous powers to intervene in the affairs of sovereign states and local communities through its projects, Country Programme Papers (CPPs), country economic missions, and Structural Adjustment Programmes (SAPs). Writing in the *Harvard Human Rights Journal*, Jonathan Cahn calls attention to the enormous power which the World Bank wields: 'Bank-approved consultants often rewrite a country's trade policy, fiscal policies, civil service requirements, labour laws, health care arrangements, environmental regulations, energy policy, resettlement requirements, procurement rules and budgetary policy.'[3] Bruce Rich also points out that the World Bank has created numerous semi-autonomous institutions like the Electric Generating Authority in Thailand (EGAT) which promote the Bank's development paradigm in their respective Third World countries.[4]

Unfortunately there are no effective structures of accountability within the Bank or adequate procedures whereby those affected by decisions taken by this powerful Washington-based institution can seek effective redress. The vast majority of people around the world were delighted to see the demise of autocratic governments in eastern Europe and many Third World countries in the late 1980s. However, many NGOs feel that the multilateral lending agencies, rather than assisting in this process, have actually undermined democratic and accountable governance.

I lived in the Philippines during the dictatorship of President Marcos, when the World Bank claimed that its lending policy was set by economic rather than political considerations. Despite the human rights record of the Marcos regime the Bank poured more than $3 billion into development projects in the Philippines. These benefited Marcos and his cronies and worked to the detriment of both industrial workers and peasant farmers. Eventually, under pressure from both the US government and the Bank, Marcos chose a Cabinet dominated by World Bank technocrats like Cesar Virata, the Prime Minister; Roberto Ongpin, the Minister for Industry; and the Central Bank Governor, Jaime Laya. These functionaries gave legitimacy to the murderous and extraordinarily corrupt regime. After the assassination of Benigno Aquino in 1983 they presided over the disintegration of the Philippine economy. In 1984 alone the GNP contracted by 5.5 per cent.

With the help of over 6,000 leaked documents Walden Bello and his co-authors tell the story of the Bank's connections with the Marcos regime in *Development Debacle: The World Bank in the Philippines*. The authors insist that the World Bank's programmes 'have directly served US, strategic and corporate interests, supported authoritarian control by a brutal dictator, and worked against the welfare of the majority of the people in the Philippines'.[5]

Support for right-wing dictators and other principles of US foreign policy were not confined to the Philippines. The Bank supported Somoza in Nicaragua and Mobutu in Zaïre. In the 1980s the Bank's lending policy matched US President Reagan's foreign policy: the military junta in El Salvador, which was fighting a bloody civil war, received constant support while neighbouring Nicaraguan Sandinistas were shut out. A bizarre comparison is the support which the Bank gave to the communist dictatorship of Nicolae Ceauşescu in Romania, in the early 1970s, and the simultaneous withdrawal of support from the democratically elected Marxist government of Salvador Allende in Chile.

Ceauşescu received support because his perceived independence from the USSR within the Warsaw Pact was viewed in a favourable light by Washington. Notwithstanding the support which the Bank's huge lending programme gave to a notorious dictator, it is worth recalling that their economic predictions were completely wrong. A 1979 Bank report on Romania was of the opinion that:

> It remains probable that Romania will continue to enjoy one of the highest growth rates among developing countries over the next decade and that it will largely succeed in implementing its development targets . . . If all plans are fulfilled Romania will have 'taken off' and become an industrialized economy by 1990, on a level with many other countries considered to be developed.[6]

Given their wide-ranging powers to intervene in a country's economic policies, especially through SAPs, and the lack of accountability, it is reasonable to ask: whose interest do the World Bank and the IMF serve? Many people – in the NGOs and citizens groups, especially in the South – feel that they have fostered policies which primarily benefit Northern construction companies and banks, the Southern élite and the World Bank itself. For example, once a World Bank loan is approved US corporations and citizens are given access to the relevant documents through a Department of Commerce reading room. This service is provided in order to assist US companies in procuring business with the Bank. No similar service is available to citizens of Third World countries even when their livelihood and residence may be threatened by World Bank-funded projects.[7]

Despite the Bank's rhetoric about alleviating poverty, the operations of the Bank are biased towards the interests of the North. Since its inception rich countries have had a stranglehold on the World Bank. In 1993 the ten richest countries controlled 52 per cent of the votes. Their power over Bank decisions is exercised through executive directors. At present there are 24 directors. Their voting power on projects is roughly equivalent to the amount of money which the country contributes to the Bank. Initially the US controlled 36 per cent of the votes. This has now slipped to 17.5 per cent. However the US has not used its diminishing share of the Bank capital to promote more democratic participation in the Bank's operations. On the contrary, in order to protect its interests the US succeeded in changing the Articles of Agreement in order to raise the percentage of votes needed for change from 80 to 85 per cent.[8]

Despite its much vaunted expertise and its ready access to economists, planners, accountants and lawyers the World Bank does not have a distinguished record of success in its projects. In 1987, out of a representative sample of 150 projects, almost 60 per cent were found to have 'serious shortcomings' or to have been 'a complete failure'.[9] Patricia Adams devotes one chapter in *Odious Debts* to examining the record of the World Bank and finds the results dismal. Economists and planners from the Bank and the IMF have repeatedly advised countries to expand the commodity base of their economies. This involved producing more rubber, cotton, iron ore, tea, coffee, tobacco and such primary commodities rather than concentrating on the added-value side of the economic equation. This resulted in production gluts for crucial commodities and a consequent fall in prices on the world markets. It would appear that the real beneficiaries of the Bank's advice are Northern TNCs and their consumers.[10]

In good commercial banking practice a bank will carefully evaluate the risks involved in making loans. No bank will lend money if it is clear that a project will not generate enough income to repay the loan and make a reasonable profit. While the World Bank is not a commercial bank and does not operate within those narrow confines, it should research more thoroughly the economic viability of the projects that it funds. Critics like Patricia Adams accuse the Bank of bad financial management. She maintains that 'if the World Bank's shareholders – 155 member countries – tried to privatize it, they would find that no private investor wanted a bank whose assets overwhelmingly consist of loans to Third World countries, most of whom need new loans to pay back their old ones'.[11]

Many NGOs are now demanding that the World Bank take some responsibility for loans which funded poorly-designed projects that have failed economically, socially and environmentally. Apart from relieving the debt burden for poor countries, such action would increase significantly accountability at the Bank. Earlier loans should be scrutinized by an international tribunal chosen by the Bank's Board of Executive Directors.

THE WORLD BANK AND THE ENVIRONMENT

The World Bank has a poor record in terms of promoting projects which are either environmentally benign or sustainable. For a long time the Bank simply ignored environmental considerations and proceeded to fund dams, hydroelectric and irrigation projects, roads and other massive infrastructural developments, many of which have lamentable environmental consequences. A 1991 review of the Bank's lending on energy programmes established that less than 1 per cent was devoted to improving end-use efficiency and other conservation measures. If actions speak louder than words no radical environmental conversion has taken place since the expenditure on end-use efficiency dropped in the late 1980s.[12]

In *Mortgaging the Earth* Bruce Rich discusses in detail three representative projects which turned out to be social and environmental disasters. Two of these, Carajas (a mining and railway development) and Polonoroeste (road building and agricultural colonization), are located in Brazil, the third is a transmigration programme in Indonesia.

Despite the fact that previous efforts to colonise the Amazon had failed dismally, and in the face of trenchant criticism from its own internal Operations Evaluation Department (OED), the Bank poured hundreds of millions of dollars into the Polonoroeste project in the 1980s. Rich maintains that Polonoroeste 'transformed Rondonia – an area approximately the size of Oregon or Great Britain – into a region with one of the highest forest destruction rates in the Brazilian Amazon'. The impact on the Amerindian population included the 'systematic pillaging of Indian lands . . . and rampant epidemics of tuberculosis, measles and malaria in the indigenous areas'.[13]

The Carajas project created much the same kind of forest devastation in the state of Para at the other end of the Amazon basin. Here the World Bank lent over $300 million in order to build a railway to transport high-grade ore to the sea. Included in the original project were plans to build 34 charcoal-burning industries to produce pig-iron along the railway corridor. The timber for producing charcoal was supposed to come from eucalyptus plantations. In fact it came from the standing forest and this has resulted in massive deforestation in the area. Despite its central involvement in the project, the World Bank attempted to shift the responsibility for what happened in Carajas to the Brazilian state mining company, Companhia Vale del Rio Doce (CVRD). Rich insists that 'the Bank's responsibility was central, since it funded the basic infrastructure (the mine, the railroad and the deep-water port) for

the devastation that followed'. Furthermore, 'the Bank's operations staff and management prevented the Bank's environmental
staff from appraising the broader adverse regional, environmental
and social consequences of the scheme'.[14]

Halfway around the world the World Bank provided over \$500
million to the Indonesian government to move millions of people
from heavily populated areas like Java and Bali to Sumatra, West
Irian and Kalimantan. The Bank embraced transmigration as a
development strategy despite the fact that human rights organizations, both inside and outside Indonesia, saw the project as a
geopolitical exercise to control indigenous people in the outer
islands. The strategy involved transporting mainly Javanese to
places like West Irian and Sumatra. Once the Javanese outnumber
the indigenous populations it will be much easier to control these
outlying areas of the Indonesian empire.

On the economic front the scheme made little sense. The Bank's
own figures put the cost of resettling a family at \$7,000. This is 'three
times the per capita income of most poor families in the inner
islands'.[15] Many of those resettled found it difficult to make a living
in their new area since the soils in the outer islands are poor and not
suitable for continuous agriculture. Transmigration has had a very
negative impact on West Irian, an area of the world which is
exceedingly rich in biological and cultural diversity. By 1990 it
produced a lot of damage and the resettlement policy was a fiasco: it
was extraordinarily expensive and rather than alleviating poverty it
had merely redistributed it, and in the process caused ecological and
social havoc.

In 1988 the World Bank decided to improve its environmental
image and record. As a sign of good intent it expanded its
environment section and promised to enhance its role in project
design. Many critics of the Bank argue that this department has not
been taken seriously. Some feel that the new-found environmental
conversion was primarily a public relations exercise, aimed at
persuading the political leaders in the run-up to the 1992 Earth
Summit in Rio to use World Bank facilities to fund environmental
projects. Furthermore, many environmentalists were furious that a
new facility termed the General Environment Facility (GEF),
which came into being after Rio, was stabled at the World Bank,
given the Bank's environmental record. It is worth noting that the
initative on GEF came not from the Bank's environment staff but

from the financial department. Rich believes that 'one of GEF's unstated functions for the Bank is sweetening the financial terms of larger Bank loan packages.'[16]

Once again the GEF proposal highlights the secrecy at the World Bank. The facility was put in place without any discussion with national parliaments, even the US Congress. NGOs who had led the way in creating a heightened environmental consciousness were not consulted. Even the Bank's environmental staff were kept in the dark. At the last moment the United Nations Development Programme (UNDP) was co-opted by the Bank in order to give the proposal respectability. Very soon its role was sidelined.[17]

World Bank officials, when challenged about the Bank's dismal environmental record, admit that in the 1960s, 1970s and early 1980s the environmental record was poor. However, they go on to claim that 'that's history' or 'the Bank is now committed to sustainable development'. They point to the Morse Report as evidence that the Bank can be self-critical and self-corrective. The Morse Report critically assessed the World Bank's role in the Narmada dam débâcle in India and yet the Bank is still funding environmentally questionable projects in early 1994.

Environmentalists predict that the World Bank-financed Pak Mun dam on the Mun river in Thailand will have harmful effects on the Mekong's fisheries. (The Mun is a tributary of the Mekong.) Three world-renowned aquatic biologists – Drs Walter Rainboth, George Davis and David Woodruff – accused the Bank of ignoring the ecological consequences of dynamiting unusual rock formations and inundating rapids which provide essential feeding grounds for migrating Mekong fish. The experts pointed out that this area is world-famous for its extraordinary diversity of fish species – over 1,000 in all. The drop in fish populations on both the Mun and the Mekong will have a harmful impact on human communities along the river banks. Thai environmental researchers have indeed documented dramatic falls in fish populations, and many families are now hungry because fish catches have dropped by 30 per cent.

The Bank has ignored this evidence. It has turned a deaf ear to persistent calls for a thorough evaluation of the project from scores of local environmental organizations and even the US executive director of the Bank. Recently, in the wake of a mid-term review, it signalled that the project will continue and plans to release the next disbursement in order to complete the dam.[18]

THE WORLD BANK AND THE DEBT CRISIS

In the early 1980s, when the debt crisis engulfed many Third World countries, the World Bank and the IMF insisted on, and often forced, Structural Adjustment Programmes (SAPs) on countries saddled with heavy debt burdens. SAPs are usually delivered in a single-size measure for all clients; however, more recently some unique features in individual countries have been taken into account. The main thrust of SAPs has been two-pronged: a package of monetary and fiscal policies aimed at stabilizing the demand side of an economy and restructuring the supply side (see Chapter 1). This is done in accordance with the prevailing canons of the neo-classical model of development.

The Bank and the Fund claim that these programmes have helped improve the economies of poor countries, even in Africa. Towards the end of 1993 the Managing Director of the IMF, Michel Camdessus, claimed that the fall in Zambia's inflation rate during the previous year from 150 per cent to almost zero was 'a remarkable achievement'. Kevin Watkins, writing in the *Guardian* (10 January 1994), adds that what 'he [Camdessus] omitted to add is that a real interest rate of 50 per cent had contributed to the virtual cessation of manufacturing investment, or to the loss of over 12,000 jobs in the textile sector alone'. Similar criticisms are made of World Bank and IMF programmes by representatives from NGOs who see the impact which these economic changes have brought about.

Everyone who saw the gaunt, emaciated bodies of starving Somalis on TV knows that an appalling tragedy took place there in the late 1980s and early 1990s. Many people in Northern countries were so horrified that they collected money in their local churches, clubs and workplaces to help the people of Somalia escape their misery. The following few statistics about life in Somalia paint a depressing picture: infant mortality is at 122 per 1,000 births, life expectancy at birth is 45 years, and the per capita GDP in 1990 was $120.

The causes of the war and famine in Somalia are complex and they have their roots in the colonial past. More recently, however, the war against Ethiopia placed enormous strains on the resources of the country. Within a few years 1 million displaced people and their cattle fled into Somalia. This influx taxed both the human and natural resources of the country. Overgrazing led to soil erosion, which in turn led to the death of many cattle and the people who were dependent on them for their food.

It was in this period of extreme adversity that the country was forced by the IMF and the World Bank to renegotiate its foreign debt. As part of this package it had to accept an IMF/World Bank-inspired adjustment programme. This did not cure Somalia's economic ills and may have exacerbated them. The national debt stock increased from $1,639 million in 1985 to $2,444 million in 1990. The scale of the burden is clear when one compares the per capita GDP in Somalia in 1990 – $120 – with the debt burden on each Somali – $281.

The adjustment policies increased the country's dependence on imported cereals. This put local maize and millet producers out of business, caused massive internal migration and changed local consumption patterns. The Somali shilling was also devalued. As a consequence the price of agricultural inputs soared. Much of the best arable land was taken over by government and military personnel. Instead of growing food crops this land was devoted to export crops: cotton, fruit, vegetables and vegetable oils. The adjustment programme also led to the collapse of cattle farming. Traditional Somali exports of cattle to Saudi Arabia were replaced by beef imports from Australia and Europe.

The adjustment programme also contributed to the disintegration of public services. Expenditure in the health sector in 1989 was 78 per cent lower than in 1975. On the education side statistics also show a 44 per cent fall in school enrolment between 1981 and 1989. The elements in the adjustment programme aimed at streamlining and reducing numbers in the public service also backfired. Wage levels collapsed in the urban areas. Real wages in the public sector in 1989 were 90 per cent lower than in 1970.

By 1989 Somalia was in a terrible state: arrears on long-term debt had reached $423 million, debt servicing was $32 million and export earnings were a mere $70 million. Instead of admitting the total failure of the adjustment programme the IMF and the World Bank decided to chastise Somalia. The IMF suspended its loans and the World Bank froze a Structural Adjustment Loan (SAL) worth $70 million. The Somalia state disintegrated. Once drought, famine and environmental degradation were thrown into the mix, the country succumbed to civil war and starvation.

The reasons for this tragic collapse are complex. They include widespread internal corruption, gross incompetence of local leaders, superpower rivalry, and an arms build-up. However one commentator is convinced that SAPs contributed significantly to Somalia's desperate plight. Marcus Arruda, a Brazilian economist and co-ordinator of the NGO group in the World Bank (Geneva), presented a paper entitled 'Structural adjustment in Somalia: a disaster' in October 1993.[19] He argued that 'The ultimate purpose of the adjustment was not to salvage the national economy and to establish a sustainable, self-reliant development process, but rather to release funds in order to service the foreign debt to the members of the Club of Paris and the IMF and World Bank themselves.'[20]

As one of the main creditors the IMF refused to reschedule the debt though it was obvious to NGOs and church agencies that a catastrophe was unfolding. The World Bank and the IMF have been reluctant to reduce or reschedule debts owed to them. They claim that this would adversely affect their ability to raise capital on the financial markets for lending programmes. Critics dismiss this and point out that the Bank and the Fund have large capital reserves ($17 billion and $35 billion respectively). At least half of this could be used to cancel the debts of severely indebted, low-income countries. This would have no effect on the credit-worthiness of either institution.

Unfortunately, the Somali experience is not unique. Since the 1980s 35 sub-Saharan African countries have come under IMF/World Bank-sponsored SAPs. A 1989 report, jointly sponsored by the World Bank and the United Nations Development Programme (UNDP), claimed that a recovery in African economies began in 1985 – the year that SAPs were widely applied.

MOUNTING CRITICISM

NGOs like Oxfam and independent economists like Charles Abugre and G. K. Helleiner dispute such claims. Two reports, released in 1992 and commissioned from within the Bank, confirm many of the criticisms which NGOs have levelled against the Bank.

The Morse Commission was chaired by Bradford Morse, a former UN Under Secretary-General, and was formed in response to national and international criticism of the World Bank-financed Sardar Sarovar dam on the Narmada river in India. The Commission members were appalled by what they discovered. Their Report documented a decade of what Bruce Rich called 'bureaucratic maleficence, willful withholding of information from the Bank's management and Board of Directors, and sheer incompetence'.[21] The Report put the number of people who would be displaced by the dam at 240,000 and not the 90,000 or 100,000 as Bank officials originally claimed. 'There appeared to have been an institutional numbness at the Bank and in India to environmental matters.'[22]

The Morse Report uncovered a pattern of deception running right through each stage of the project. When the executive directors approved the $450 million in loans and credits for Sardar Sarovar in 1985 they were unaware that the project was only viable as part of a larger development which would necessitate the construction of even more ecologically and socially damaging dams, especially at Narmada Sagar.[23] The Morse Commission concluded that 'The Bank is more concerned to accommodate pressures emanating from its borrowers than to guarantee implementation of its policies'.[24]

Despite such criticism the Bank decided to continue funding the Sardar Sarovar dam. Even though the World Bank commissioned the Morse Report it ignored or reinterpreted many of its recommendations. So serious was this matter that Morse felt compelled to write to Lewis Preston, the President of the Bank, in October 1992. He complained that a report sent by Preston to the Board of the Bank 'ignores or misrepresents the main findings of the review'.[25]

For another report a vice-president of the Bank, Willi Wapenhans, was asked to review the Bank's record in a variety of projects which it had financed over the years. Using normal indicators to judge the economic rate of return and the acceptable level of compliance with loan conditions, his Report admitted that the quality of the Bank's loan portfolio was deteriorating dramatically. This was due to a marked increase in unsatisfactory projects, increasing from 15 per cent in 1981 to 37.5 per cent in 1991.[26]

The Wapenhans Report accepted that the pressure to promote a loan was often more to do with an individual staff member's promotion prospects than with the desirability or success of the loan on the ground: 'Management are consistently seen by staff to focus on lending targets rather than results on the ground.'[27] The Wapenhans Report also acknowledged that many projects were initiated and carried out without significant or worthwhile local input. Finally, the World Bank was seldom challenged to account for the high rate of project failure.

In the light of such reports the World Bank is under enormous pressure to reform its top-down paradigm of development. There are calls for more participation by those affected by projects, and more transparency and accountability in all its procedures. A much wider framework of participation is needed if the World Bank is to fulfil its role of fostering appropriate, sustainable development and combating widespread poverty. The Wapenhans Report recognized that even the input from government officials in borrower countries is very often not taken seriously. The involvement of NGOs and citizens groups is still only in its infancy.[28] Jonathan Cahn, writing in the *Harvard Human Rights Journal* on the World Bank, recommended that a watchdog agency be created to report on, monitor and intervene in the World Bank's lending processes. In order to be effective and credible the agency would need to be independent of the World Bank. Finally, the Church, as a moral community, should add its voice to this chorus of criticism by those who are demanding fundamental changes at the World Bank.

THE IMF: ECONOMIC INTENTIONS AND REALITY

The IMF also emerged from the Bretton Woods conference held in the summer of 1944. The Fund was created by people who had experienced the monetary chaos of the late 1920s which gave rise to the Great Depression. This multilateral financial agency was designed to maintain the smooth functioning of the global economy, through regulating the volume of international liquidity and ensuring the stability of exchange rates.

While the World Bank and the IMF often work in tandem, the specific function of the IMF is to provide short-term loans to countries which run into a balance-of-payments problem. Each member country of the IMF pays a certain amount of money, in its own currency, into the Fund. This entitles it to borrow an equivalent amount, in any currency, when faced with a temporary 'foreign exchange' crisis. If, however, a country wishes to borrow more than its allotted quota it must submit itself to strict monetary and fiscal policies which bear the IMF stamp of approval. In the original vision the IMF was geared to deal with the short-term balance-of-payment problems of industrialized countries; it was not designed to address the challenges which so-called 'development' policies have thrown up for Southern countries during the past two decades.

Throughout the 1960s and 1970s much more attention was paid to the activities of the World Bank than of the IMF. All that changed in August 1982 when Mexico ignited the Third World debt crisis by threatening to default on its loans. Fearful that the repercussions might sink the international financial system, the IMF stepped in and organized new commercial loans to head off the threatened defaults. In return the IMF insisted on deep cuts in public spending and a host of other reforms based on neo-liberal economics. These included promoting trade liberalization, the abolition of subsidies on agriculture inputs and food, and a reduction in government spending on health, social welfare, education and housing.

Over 70 countries in all have adopted IMF-designed SAPs during the past decade. In theory these loans and accompanying policies are supposed to increase long-term economic productivity and State efficiency and promote a favourable balance of payments, thereby facilitating economic growth and prosperity. Marijke Torfs, a senior policy analyst with Friends of the Earth, reviewed a document published by the IMF on the impact of SAPs. She found that 'adjustment measures have put the heaviest burden of adjustment on the shoulders of the poor due to a combination of factors: declining wages, increasing unemployment, a significant price rise of basic consumer goods and devaluations of the national currency'.[29]

This is borne out by experience in countries as diverse as Zimbabwe and the Philippines where SAPs have led to increased poverty and widespread environmental destruction. Dr Leonor Briones, the President of the Philippine Freedom From Debt Coalition, described SAPs in the Philippines as 'adjusting people out of jobs, homes, schools, and in extreme cases, out of existence'.[30] Christian Aid reports that in Jamaica SAPs have led to cuts in spending on education, health and social welfare. As a result child malnutrition has risen steadily since 1980. Women have paid a heavy price for SAPs. 'Information currently being collected by Oxfam and other NGOs throughout the developing world strongly suggests that it is women who pay the highest price in the labour force, in the home and in the community for this economic crisis: paying with their time, their energy and their health.'[31]

Neither should one overlook the fact that the IMF has used SAPs to promote the globalization of the world's economy, thus facilitating the entry of foreign capital and corporations into the Third World economy. The pressure to privatize government enterprises seldom involves the need to modernize equipment and streamline bureaucracy or develop local self-reliance. Rather it has often led to the collapse of indigenous industries and opened the way for TNCs to move into the void. In such an economic climate TNCs benefit from the wage freeze which usually accompanies SAPs. In the aftermath of IMF-designed SAPs for India in the late 1980s, Bata, the multinational shoe manufacturer, decided to lay off many permanent unionized workers. These people were normally paid 80 rupees ($3.20) per day. In the new arrangement Bata subcontracted the work to independent shoemakers who are paid a mere 25 rupees (less than $1) per day.[32]

The 1993 Oxfam report *The Failure of IMF/World Bank Policies in Africa* makes the same point. In a stinging attack on current IMF/ World Bank policies it states that:

> After a decade of structural adjustment programmes (SAPs), implemented under the tutelage of the World Bank and the International Monetary Fund (IMF), Africa remains trapped in a downward spiral of economic and social decline. Hard-won gains in health and education have been reversed; living standards are in decline; poverty is increasing; and the crisis is set to deepen.

The report calls on governments in the North to drop their ritualistic support for policies which have done so much damage and instead to demand 'an open review of what has gone wrong'. The authors of the report recognize that there are other external and internal causes for the significant decline in living standards across Africa, but they are unwavering in indicting the monetarist policies of the IMF/World Bank for exacerbating the situation.

At the very moment when Zimbabwe was emerging from the effects of a devastating drought and should have been gently nudged back to economic health the IMF moved in. Its stabilization programme concentrated on putting out the fires of inflation. This fire-brigade action fuelled rises in interest rates which proved a major deterrent to the likelihood of an investment-led recovery. The results of these poorly conceived policies have been high levels of unemployment and industries operating at a fraction of their capacity. Many, in fact, have collapsed. The combined effect of drought and SAPs has produced a dramatic increase in infant mortality in Zimbabwe: from 23 per 1,000 live births to 43 per 1,000. No wonder the Finance Minister in Zimbabwe called the IMF policies 'monetary terrorism', and that they have been excoriated by a coalition ranging from the Chambers of Commerce to church leaders and NGOs.

The Oxfam report also criticized the way both the World Bank and the IMF have handled the debt crisis in Africa. The total debt burden in sub-Saharan Africa has tripled since 1980 and stood at $183 billion in late 1993. Debt servicing now eats up a quarter of combined export earnings or around $10 billion per annum. The report states that 'both [IMF/World Bank] have approached the issue with a degree of complacency which, in view of the profound social and economic implications of continued inertia on debt relief, can only be described as irresponsible' (p. 8).

In sub-Saharan Africa Oxfam accuses the IMF of negative financial transfers out of the region to the level of $3 billion since 1983. Reminiscent of the worst excesses of the Conquistadores in South America in the sixteenth century, this multilateral financial agency is draining the life from an area of the world which has experienced pain, destruction and death during the past two decades. The countries of sub-Saharan Africa will never get on their feet while such haemorrhaging is allowed to continue.

Oxfam has called on Northern governments, who fund the IMF and the World Bank, to create a fund to write off this debt through the sale of a fraction of the IMF gold reserves (currently valued at $35 billion). Further, Oxfam recommends that the IMF and World Bank should actively support the Trinidad Terms in order to demonstrate that they see the resolution of the debt crisis as crucial to the prosperity in the South.[33] The Trinidad Terms envisage the writing off of two-thirds of the entire stock of debt for the most severely indebted, mainly African countries and the rescheduling of the remainder of the debt over a period of 25 years. The terms refer to bilateral debts which were contracted before the country's initial agreement with the Club of Paris.

TWO CASE STUDIES

An editorial in the *Guardian* (13 April 1994) severely criticized the myopia of the IMF's policies in Algeria. Algeria is one of the countries in North Africa poised on the brink of a revolution promoted by Islamic fundamentalist religious groups. The editorial asks:

> With friends like the IMF, how can Algeria cope with its enemies? The statement by Michel Camdessus [the IMF Managing Director] on Algeria's enforced decision to devalue was a myopic masterpiece. Devaluation, he said on Monday, should allow the Algerian economy to 'achieve high growth, particularly in housing and industry, renew job creation, and bring down the rate of inflation'. For someone who knows perfectly well the complexity of these issues in the most

favourable circumstances, and the mixed record – to put it mildly – of IMF-imposed policies elsewhere, this is not prediction but unashamed PR. It is further undercut by Mr Camdessus's failure even to mention the dire political context.

These hardships, so soon after the recent increases in the price of milk, bread and other essential commodities, will impose heavy burdens on Algerians and may drive more and more young people into the arms of the banned Islamic Salvation Front. Unfortunately, nobody is likely to lose their jobs in the IMF when policies they have imposed on Algeria reap a whirlwind of violence.

In response to criticisms by development agencies like Oxfam and UNICEF, Michel Camdessus has insisted that more recent SAPs must include a segment on the 'social dimension of adjust-ment' (SDAs) in order to protect the most vulnerable groups in society. The NGOs' analysis of such programmes does not lead one to believe that change will occur. The Oxfam report found that even the most recent SAPs have been poorly designed, inadequately monitored and often derailed in bureaucratic bungles. In the final analysis they have not substantially mitigated the destructive impact of the Fund's monetarist policies.

IMF failures are not confined to Third World countries. Harvard economics professor Jeffrey D. Sachs, in a *Washington Post* article (4 March 1994) entitled 'The IMF's phony figures on aid to Russia', writes that 'as the International Monetary Fund tries to conceal its massive failures in Russia, its obfuscations grow more desperate'. He challenges Michel Camdessus's claim that Western aid to Russia amounted to $58 billion over the two years of 1992–93. This figure includes $31 billion arising from Russia's non-payment of old debts contracted by the former USSR. Another $4 billion, paid by Germany to relocate Soviet troops, is also included despite an agreement not to include this as part of the Western aid package. Camdessus's calculations throw in another $20 billion, which supposedly comes from Western governments.

'Not so', says Sachs. 'First the total itself is dubious and not documented by the IMF.' Secondly, most of the total was trade credits that Russia is obliged to repay at market rates, much of it within a short period of time. Thirdly, as the IMF knows well, the trade credits were not part of any assistance package for reforms. Various governments tried to sell their surplus merchandise to Russia – Italian shoes, East German antiquated machinery – and they did this with the incentive of short-term loans to Russia's corrupt and profligate State trading companies. The companies took the goods and the Russian budget got the debts. Third World countries in the 1970s were led down this slippery path to the debt crisis of the 1980s.

Sachs concedes that the IMF challenged this practice. But he finds it ridiculous that Camdessus presents these trade credits as part of the Western aid package. Sachs estimates that only $2 billion of the $20 billion from Western governments came in the form of grants rather than loans, despite the political and military consequences of a collapse in Russia. It is worth recalling that both the IMF and the World Bank profess to be interested in development and political stability. Nevertheless they only contributed $2 billion to help Russia make the transition from a Marxist, centrally planned economy to a free-market economy. In summary, Sachs maintains that 'Western aid effort has been disgraceful: almost no grants, self-serving short-term trade credits, virtually no support from the IMF and World Bank . . . and continued preening about our help'.

THE IMF AND THE ENVIRONMENT

One area where IMF policy has been particularly weak is in adding environmental considerations into its macroeconomic policies. Unlike the World Bank, the IMF has not conducted studies on the possible environmental consequences of its programmes and does not see this as a major oversight. Despite pressure from environmental groups like Friends of the Earth the IMF's executive directors decided not to set up an environment unit within the Fund in February 1991. By 1992 however, with the Earth Summit on the horizon, Michel Camdessus was beginning to sound a little Greener. In a speech at the United Nations Conference on Environment and Development (UNCED) Mr Camdessus declared that 'Any growth strategy, to be sustainable, must respect the environment; and environmental protection, to be effective, has to be a part of a viable growth strategy . . . '.

Following this, in May 1993, the IMF hosted a conference for NGOs on macroeconomic policies and the environment. At this the IMF's environmental rhetoric appeared very shallow. There was a fundamental divergence between the position of NGO participants and IMF officials. The former stressed the need for an integrated approach to social, economic and environmental problems, while the latter insisted that the IMF's primary role was to help IMF member countries adopt economic policies which would stabilize their economies in the short term.

Little wonder then that the IMF-inspired programmes are unable to address environmental issues. According to Robert Repetto of the World Resource Institute SAPs are inadequate to deal with the problems facing most Third World countries.[34] Repetto insists that the standard IMF macroeconomic framework does not consider the 'links between macroeconomic policy and environmental degradation'. Even some of the necessary tools to facilitate this, like natural resource accounting systems, are lacking in the standard national income accounts of most countries.

Repetto believes that the most pressing problem facing many Third World countries is not simply their foreign debt crisis but the constant deterioration in their natural resources. He estimates that in the Philippines there was a 4.5 per cent annual depreciation in forests, soils and coastal fisheries in the decade leading up to the debt crisis. SAPs intensified this destruction by driving hundreds of thousands of people from the rural areas into urban slums. Alternatively they migrated to the fragile ecological watershed areas or mangrove forests. In another example, pressure from the World Bank and IMF on Ghana has resulted in an increase in tropical timber exports, necessitated by the need to meet its debt repayments. The long-term ecological damage of such plunder is worrying. The harsh conditions which the IMF also imposed on Zambia, Zimbabwe and Uganda have caused environmental damage.

Herman Daly, formerly of the World Bank and a pioneer in environmental economics, has called for significant changes in the macroeconomic framework of the IMF. He regards it as an accounting error to treat, solely as income, the kind of ecological depletion which is taking place in many countries like Ghana and Sudan. In a paper co-authored with John Kellenberg, he points out that both the World Bank and the IMF normally exclude the opportunity cost of depleted natural capital in project evaluation. This, of course, overstates the rate of return on projects that deplete natural capital. This leads to a bias where 'too many resources will be allocated to projects which deplete natural capital, while too few resources are allocated to restorative and sustainable-yield projects'.[35]

A similar omission can be found in balance-of-payments accounting when the export of non-renewable resources or the over-exploitation of renewable resources is placed in the current rather than capital account. Because the harvesting of these resources is unsustainable some portion of non-sustainable exports should be treated as the sale of a capital asset. Kellenberg and Daly rightly point out that 'counting capital consumption as if it were income is the greatest of all accounting sins'.[36]

Such a change in accounting procedures would have far-reaching implications for the development policies of the IMF:

> If this [accounting] were properly done, some countries would see their apparent balance-of-trade surplus converted into a true deficit, one that was being financed by the draw-down and transfer abroad of their stock of natural capital. Reclassifying transactions in a way that converts a country's balance of trade from a surplus to a deficit would trigger a whole different set of IMF recommendations and actions. This reform of accounting procedures might well be the initial focus of the IMF's new interest in environmentally sustainable development.[37]

Finally, Repetto contends that adjustment programmes must be designed to reduce the debt burden and, at the same time, lessen the depreciation of ecological capital. Ecological damage often stems from pricing and taxation policies which make the exploitation of natural resources artificially cheap. Repetto claims that 'proper pricing of natural resources . . . fulfils four complementary objectives: reducing government deficits, improving the productivity of the economy, reducing ecological damage and reducing concentration of income'.[38]

ESSENTIAL REFORMS

Many critics doubt whether the international financial institutions can actually reform themselves since such reforms would be strenuously opposed by vested interests and political élites. Rather than addressing the concerns raised by environmentalists, development workers, journalists or economists and responding to them in an effective way, the IMF, like its sister institution the World Bank, has decided to go on the offensive with a public relations campaign. In September 1993 it published *Ten Misconceptions About the IMF*. The text is full of bland generalizations such as: 'The IMF as a matter of explicit policy does not take a position on social or politicial issues, but works within the existing sociopolitical systems in member countries.'[39] The experience of government officials in Algeria, Nicaragua, the Philippines or India scarcely supports this statement.

The environmental NGO Friends of the Earth has spearheaded a campaign in the US to promote reforms at the IMF and World Bank. Among these structural reforms are the creation of a special audit department which would include experts in the environment and poverty-reduction endowed with broad powers to review all IMF programmes and activities; the establishment of an environment and social unit, preferably in the Fiscal Affairs Department. In the light of the poor environmental and social record of the IMF, it is essential to have a senior environment expert in the office of the Managing Director to ensure that environmentally sound policies are vigorously promoted. The management of the IMF should also promote Policy Framework Papers (PFPs) which could be used to examine the implications of integrating environmental concerns into the general conditions of loan approvals.

In recent years Friends of the Earth attempted to focus its call for reforms around a campaign designed to block an IMF appropriation bill in the US Congress unless extensive reforms were put in place. The campaign was not completely successful: Congress approved the measure when the Bush administration incorporated a Russian aid package into the legislation. Nevertheless, the legislation requires the US executive director to support many of the above recommendations, expecially the incorporation of poverty alleviation and environmental considerations into all future IMF programmes.

In terms of transparency and accountability both the IMF and the World Bank must promote greater public participation in their activities. During the 1980s decisions were taken about economic management in a highly centralized and non-participatory manner. Very often only the Ministry of Finance, the Central Bank and the Office of the President in a particular country were involved in the decision-making. However, ministries that impinge on the lives of people – like the Ministries of Health, Education or Welfare – were often unaware of what was happening and therefore unable to deal with the consequences of decisions taken in secret. Middle-level staff members of the IMF and the World Bank were more likely to know the pros and cons of the policy alternatives under consideration in individual African countries than the nationals of those countries. This has often given these programmes the pejorative tag

'made-in-Washington'.[40] In an *Ecologist* article Michel Chossudovsky recalls that a World Bank report on the Indian economy was
held back from the then Prime Minister and the Cabinet Secretary
by a group of eight officials who had been associated with the World
Bank or IMF.[41] The author maintains that the IMF has direct access
to all crucial economic data in India and it is using its power, through
the SAPs, to bypass democratic institutions and effectively decide
India's economic policy.

Resentment at foreign bullying abounds among technocrats who
might share the IMF/World Bank economic viewpoint, but especially among community and church groups and NGOs. In this kind
of climate it is little wonder that many of the programmes are seen
as narrow and inappropriate and consequently not 'owned' by local
people. A 1993 UNDP report on technical co-operation involved in
designing and implementing SAPs is devastating as it shows it to be
costly and inefficient.[42]

The multilateral agencies must work to change the development
framework and their operating procedures if they wish to devise
programmes which will suit individual countries and have the
whole-hearted support of local people. One way of doing this is to
take seriously the suggestions of bona fide NGOs from both the
development and environment lobbies. The churches should also
lend their moral support to organizations like Friends of the Earth
who are lobbying for such fundamental changes. In his encyclical
Sollicitudo Rei Socialis (*Social Concerns*), published in 1988, Pope
John Paul II urges people 'to denounce the existence of economic,
financial and social mechanisms which accentuate the situation of
wealth for some and poverty for the rest' (no. 16).

On the threshold of the 50th anniversary of the Bretton Woods
conference it is clear to many Third World people and NGOs that
radical reform is needed at both the IMF and the World Bank. Their
policies must be thoroughly revised so that they will begin to
genuinely alleviate the grinding poverty which is the lot of hundreds
of millions of people and at the same time support sustainable
development. Given the poor record of the World Bank and the
IMF in these areas, the '50 Years Is Enough' campaign will attempt
to address a variety of audiences. It will try to enlist the support of
the media to bring the glare of publicity to bear on the Bank and the
Fund. It will also challenge national governments to take a much
more active role in the functions of these institutions, since
ultimately they are dependent on taxpayers' money. The coalition
of NGOs involved is also advocating much more open and

accountable institutions that promote socially and environmentally responsible development.

The World Bank has a moral responsibility to address the grievances of the 2 to 3 million poor people who have been displaced by World Bank projects. Most of these people have never been properly compensated or resettled. Furthermore, individual governments should seek alternative institutions through which to channel foreign assistance to Third World countries. Member governments of the World Bank/IMF must also be challenged by their citizens to insist these institutions become more accountable and responsive to genuine needs.

On the Third World debt, the campaign recommends that the debt owed to the IMF by severely indebted low-income countries (those with a per capita GDP below $675) should be cancelled entirely. The terms for severely indebted middle-income countries (those with GDP between $675 and $2,695) should enjoy a 50 per cent write-off in debts to the IMF.

Most people find it repugnant that poor countries like the Philippines have to repay debts which were contracted under very questionable circumstances by dictators like President Marcos. Since both the World Bank and the IMF have played key roles in the debt crisis these institutions should work to establish a minimal standard that must be met so that the international debt obligations of a government are deemed to be legitimate and therefore enforceable under the provisions of international law. David Korten of The People-Centered Development Forum in New York has drawn up such a list of conditions. These include:

The borrowing government have an established procedure for the negation and acceptance of foreign debt obligations that conforms to the standards of the international convention as approved by an elected legislative body with constitutional responsibility for financial appropriations.

The basic details of each loan agreement must be published in leading newspapers at least 60 days before signing and all relevant documentation must be published and readily available for review in readily accessible public locations by any interested person.

The responsible administrative agency must hold publicized, open public hearings at which responsible officials solicit public input and respond to questions.

There should be provisions for international sanctions against any lending institution that attempts to pressure governments to pay an obligation declared odious by these standards in an appropriate court of law.[43]

Whether bureaucracies as large as the IMF or the World Bank can adapt in an effective way to the real needs of poor people and the environment is open to question. The Bank's inability to take on board constructive criticism is highlighted in its response to Bruce Rich's book *Mortgaging the Earth*. The *New York Times* (2 March 1994) reported that instead of examining Rich's criticisms the director of the Bank's External Affairs department, Alexander Shakow, circulated a memo to senior Bank officials demanding a rebuttal of the main thesis of Rich's book. The memo read: 'The President's office places a high priority on the speedy and effective preparations of the Bank's views in a readable and easily-used form.' This does not give much grounds for optimism that the Bank is considering serious changes in its development philosophy or in its procedures and processes.

Once again the poor, who constitute the majority of people especially in the South, are being denied access to a sufficient portion of the goods of the earth which are needed to support life in some dignity. The churches must look critically at the record of the multilateral lending agencies like the World Bank and the IMF. Despite their utterances about relieving poverty they serve the interests of the rich North and the élite in the South. Many of the projects which they have funded and promoted undermine the ability of the majority of people in the South to meet their basic needs. Churches should take a moral and religious stance and promote a Jubilee year of debt forgiveness, as portrayed in Leviticus 25, during the final years of this millennium.

NOTES

1 Bruce Rich, *Mortgaging the Earth: The World Bank, Environmental Impoverishment and the Crisis of Development* (Boston: Beacon Press, 1994). See also Walden Bello, David Kinley and Elaine Elinson, *Development Debacle: The World Bank in the Philippines* (San Francisco: Institute for Food and Development Policy, 1982).
2 Mark Tran, 'Bentsen in searing World Bank attack', *Guardian* (27 April 1994), p. 16.
3 Jonathan Cahn, 'Challenging the new imperial authority: the World Bank and the democratization of development', *Harvard Human Rights Journal*, vol. 6 (1993), p. 160.

4 Bruce Rich, op. cit., p. 10: 'EGAT is largely a World Bank creation; in fact, back in the late 1950s, the Bank insisted that the Thai government create an autonomous, independent power agency, which later became EGAT, as a condition for future loans. The Bank was not only directly responsible for EGAT's birth, it was EGAT's main source of external financing, and thus exercised an important influence on its attention – or lack of attention – to environmental and social matters over the years.' Under pressure from the Bank EGAT-like institutions have mushroomed in many countries in the South. Cf. pp. 41 and 227.

5 Walden Bello et al., op. cit., p. 10.

6 Quoted in Bruce Rich, op. cit., p. 101.

7 Jonathan Cahn, op. cit., pp. 165–6.

8 Bruce Rich, op. cit., p. 58.

9 Ibid., p. 160.

10 Patricia Adams, *Odious Debts* (London: Earthscan Publications, 1991), p. 70.

11 Ibid., p. 72.

12 Bruce Rich, op. cit., p. 170.

13 Ibid., pp. 26–9, 171–5.

14 Ibid., pp. 31, 173.

15 Ibid., p. 35.

16 Ibid., p. 175.

17 Ibid., p. 176.

18 A critique of the World Bank's involvement in the Pak Mun dam is contained in *Probe International Update Service on World Bank Activities* (25 January 1994).

19 Marcus Arruda, 'Structural adjustment in Somalia: a disaster'. This paper was submitted as a contribution to the NGO–World Bank Committee debate on Structural Adjustment. The author draws on the paper of Michel Chossudovsky, 'Dépendance alimentaire, "ignorance humanitaire" en Somalie', *Le Monde Diplomatique* (July 1993), pp. 16–17.

20 Marcus Arruda, op. cit., p. 21. 'Club of Paris' refers to meetings of the Finance Ministries of the OECD countries where discussions on bilateral debt reduction take place. The group is chaired by the French Finance Minister: hence the name.

21 Bruce Rich, 'The World Bank after 50 years: no more money without total institutional reform', *Environmental Defense Fund* (October 1993), p. 6.

22 Quoted from the Morse Commission Report in Bruce Rich, 'The World Bank after 50 years', p. 6.

23 Bruce Rich, *Mortgaging the Earth*, p. 252.

24 Quoted from *Sardar Sarovar: Report of the Independent Review* in Bruce Rich, *Mortgaging the Earth*, p. 253.

25 Quoted in Bruce Rich, 'The World Bank after 50 years', p. 8.

26 Quoted from the Wapenhans Report, Task Force 4, in Bruce Rich, *Mortgaging the Earth*, p. 9.

27 Quoted from the Wapenhans Report in Jonathan Cahn, op. cit., p. 182.

28 *The World Bank Annual Report 1992*, pp. 100–1. It describes a consultation process with NGOs about policies relating to forestry projects.

29 Marijke Torfs, *Effects of the IMF Structural Adjustment Programmes on Social Sectors of the Third World Countries* (Friends of the Earth/Environmental Policy Institute/Oceanic Society, 1994), p. 15.

30 Quoted in Christina Herman, 'The IMF: Global financial policeman', *Beyond Debt*, a newsletter of the Missionary Society of St Columban's Campaign on Debt and Development Alternatives (November 1993). This section on the IMF draws heavily on Christina's research.

31 Oxfam report, *The Impact of Structural Adjustment Programmes on Women* (March 1994), p. 3.

32 Michel Chossudovsky, 'India under IMF rule', *The Ecologist* (November/December 1992), p. 272.

33 The Trinidad Terms were presented by John Major to a Commonwealth Conference in Trinidad in 1989.

34 Robert Repetto, 'Designing sustainable macroeconomic adjustment policies', private circulation (1993).

35 John Kellenberg and Herman Daly, 'Counting user cost in evaluating projects involving depletion of natural capital: World Bank best practice and beyond', private circulation (1994), p. 1.

36 Ibid., p. 2.

37 Herman Daly, 'Farewell lecture to the World Bank' (unpublished: 14 January 1994).

38 Robert Repetto, op. cit.

39 *Ten Misconceptions About the IMF* (Washington DC: External Relations Department, International Monetary Fund, 1993), p. 10.

40 G. K. Helleiner, 'From adjustment to development in sub-Saharan Africa, an overview', p. 6. This is the first chapter of a forthcoming book edited by Giovanni Andrea and Gerry Helleiner, to be published by Macmillan.

41 Michel Chossudovsky, 'India under IMF rule', p. 175.

42 Ibid., p. 10.

43 David C. Korten, *A Convention for International Lending Standards* (New York: The People-Centered Development Forum, 1993).

CHAPTER **5**

Controlling interests:
the power of TNCs

ONE WAY OF DEFLECTING any scrutiny from those who are really responsible for destroying the earth and impoverishing people is to subscribe to a kind of ecological 'Original Sin', where everyone is considered culpable. When everyone is blamed for something then no one or no specific group can be held responsible. Most people would be furious if revisionist historians decided effectively to exonerate Hitler and the Nazi party, in the case of the Holocaust, by spreading the blame thinly over all Germans or all Europeans. Yet this is exactly what happens when the 'all men have sinned' approach is adopted in environmental matters.

It means, in effect, that the T'boli people – the tribal people with whom I lived in the Philippines – are as responsible for the destruction of the earth as those who create toxic chemicals and market them aggressively. And yet the T'boli people and most tribal peoples have lived in a sustainable way within their environment for hundreds and sometimes thousands of years. Their way of life and their environment, however, have in recent decades been ravaged by the process which many corporate executives would call 'development'. This, in turn, has benefited many people – the majority of people in the North, the monied élite in the South and, especially, the corporate world. It has not necessarily benefited the T'boli. So who is really responsible?

Transnational Corporations (TNCs) need an effective critique from community groups, NGOs and the churches. TNCs are the most important economic and commercial institutions in the modern world. They have their roots in the state-chartered corporations which were promoted in the colonial world from the sixteenth century onwards. The crucial element in these newly established trading corporations was the notion of limited liability. A shareholder could not be held liable for an amount greater than his or her investment. This limiting liability encouraged traders and colonists to take risks. Even if, for example, a ship was lost and one's venture failed, one could always try again.

The transnational phase of modern corporations began to expand dramatically after the Civil War in the US. With a firm legal framework to underpin them they could mobilize capital on an unprecedented scale, 'opening wide the floodgates for horizontal and vertical integration of corporate structures'.[1]

TNCs favour large organizations and seek to gain a monopoly over important segments of the economy. Much of the expansion of TNCs in the last decade of the nineteenth and the first decade of the twentieth centuries was achieved through mergers and take-overs. This corporate-marriage fever was repeated on a number of occasions in succeeding decades, most recently in the 1980s (when deals were often built on the sandy foundations of junk bonds). The result has been an enormous growth in monopoly dominance in key industries – energy, tobacco, chemicals, steel, agribusiness, pharmaceuticals, aviation and beverages.

In the 1990s TNCs dominate and control large sections of the world economy and as a consequence wield enormous political and economic power. General Motors, for example, is the world's largest corporation. It has an income similar to Austria, which itself has the world's 21st largest Gross Domestic Product.[2] The annual sales of the tobacco giant Philip Morris exceed the GDP of New Zealand. In the decades since World War II the lion's share of commodity trading has passed through the hands of fewer than ten multi-commodity trading companies, giving them enormous power to set prices. These institutions are no longer minor players with minimal impact on the world economic or ecological scene, they are now the major players. The top 500 corporations, for example, control almost a third of global GNP and 70 per cent of world trade. In the United States the top 500 corporations own 76 per cent of all US industrial assets.[3]

TNCs are active right around the world but their power centres are in the North. Their enormous political power often shapes national and global trading policies. In fact, as John Cavanagh and Richard Barnet point out in an article in *Third World Resurgence*: 'The balance of power in world politics has shifted in recent years from territorially bound governments to companies that roam the world. As the hopes and pretentions of governments shrink almost everywhere, these imperial corporations are occupying public space and exerting a more profound influence over the lives of ever larger numbers of people.'[4]

In Chapter 2 I pointed out that TNCs were the driving force pushing towards a completion of the Uruguay Round of GATT. They saw this agreement as providing them with easier and cheaper access to commodities and a greater control of the world's markets, an ideal climate for global expansion and increased profits. The corporations assert that hefty profits are essential in order to employ more people. The record shows, however, that their increased profits do not translate into sustainable jobs. Between 1980 and 1990 the profits for the 'Fortune 500' group of companies jumped from $81.1 to $93.3 billion, an increase of over $12 billion. During this period these companies shed 3.5 million jobs.[5]

The down side of corporate expansion is that TNCs have demolished viable local and national businesses. They do not cohabit peacefully with small, local endeavours: they prefer to gobble them up. Once TNCs have seen off the effective local competition they make economic and commercial decisions with scant regard for the local or national consequences of their actions. Corporations can virtually blackmail local or national governments and workers on a number of fronts. Often they insist on banishing unions or significantly weakening workers' organizations. They can also play off one country against another and hold out for huge tax concessions in order to minimize their tax bill. An Irish example illustrates how effective this kind of blackmail can be.

In February 1994 the management of De Beers' industrial diamond factory in Shannon insisted that the workers at the plant accept a 10 per cent wage cut. The reason given by the management was that the company had run into financial difficulties due to the prolonged international recession and competition from companies in the former Soviet Union. When the workers threatened strike action the management announced that 'production currently carried out at Shannon will run the risk of being transferred elsewhere' (*Irish Press*, 9 February 1994) unless the workers accepted the management's terms. The closure of the plant would throw close to 600 people out of work and mean a loss of IR£45 million for the local economy. Very few workers can withstand this kind of pressure, which comes from both management and the local community.

Needless to say, decisions on whether to open or close a factory are seldom taken in consultation with local workers or community and political leaders. They are often taken in the secrecy of boardrooms located halfway around the world, where the directors neither know nor care about the impact on the workers. Ultimately, the eyes of most directors are on the bottom line of increased profits and not on the personal and social dislocation which might follow a factory closure.

Many of these choices have an extremely detrimental impact on the lives of individuals and communities. The workers who are made redundant may find it difficult, and in some situations impossible, to find alternative work. Mortgage holders are put in danger of losing their homes when they are unable to keep up with their payments. The knock-on impact on schools, churches and community facilities can be deadly as the quality of community life in a neighbourhood deteriorates. Many vibrant communities in Ireland and elsewhere have felt the icy winds of such decisions in recent years.

THE ENVIRONMENT AND PR

The growing power of TNCs has also had a negative impact on the environment. Many TNCs have made fortunes producing ozone-depleting chemicals or poisonous pesticides, destroying forests, depleting fertile soils, overfishing the oceans, and manufacturing cancer-causing substances like tobacco. The PR people who manage their public images would like the public to forget these facts. The media, print and electronic, have done too little to expose the facts about TNCs, and in many ways pander to their interests as they rely on them for much of their advertising revenue.

In a classic David and Goliath clash it has fallen to poorly funded community groups and a variety of NGOs to point the finger at the irresponsible environmental behaviour of TNCs. Despite meagre resources NGOs have been successful in a number of campaigns in recent years. However, this has not led to dramatic conversions in the corporate sector. But it has provoked a counter-attack. The corporate world has become worried by bad publicity and in response has released a barrage of slick publicity aimed at convincing the public that they are socially responsible and environmentally aware. Corporations such as McDonald's, Shell, British Nuclear Fuels and Dow Chemicals have attempted to wrap themselves in a Green mantle.

Under the tutelage of PR experts like Burson-Marsteller they have effectively learned the language and vocabulary of 'Greenwash'. In its glossy brochure Burson-Marsteller assures its prospective clients that it can effectively help them to manage a variety of issues, including environmental ones, before legislative and regulatory bodies, in the media and in local communities. Burson-Marsteller has a lot of expertise in managing public relations campaigns for disreputable clients. During the reign of Nicolae Ceauşescu it promoted Romania as a good place to do business. It was also hired by the military junta in Argentina, during the 'dirty war' in the 1970s, to improve the government's image abroad and to attract investment. The company was retained by A. H. Robins, the producers of the damaging inter-uterine device the Dalkon Shield, and also by Exxon after the *Exxon Valdez* disaster in Prince Edward Sound in 1989.

It was only to be expected that the corporate world would bring its new-found Greenwash rhetoric to the Rio Earth Summit in June 1992. They were ably abetted by the Secretary-General of the Earth Summit, the Canadian Maurice Strong, who incidentally made his millions in the gas and oil business. He appointed a Swiss billionaire industrialist, Stephan Schmidheiny, to act as a liaison between manufacturing and business interests. A special entity, the Business Council for Sustainable Development (BCSD), was established with representatives from over 50 TNCs. These included some of the world's most notorious polluters. Since money was no object BCSD could afford to employ Burson-Marsteller to defend interests and brush up its Green image.[6]

The Burson-Marsteller PR staff had a twofold objective at Rio. On the positive side they wished to convince the media and world public opinion that the corporate world was now willing to take the environment seriously. This was mainly about image and not substance. There are very few instances of a corporation which has been involved in destructive practices actually changing direction. The second objective was to block any agreement that might commit companies to specific requirements on environmental issues.

Burson-Marsteller helped BCSD to produce a report which encouraged industry to be more sensitive to environmental issues – to use energy and resources wisely and to avoid creating toxic substances. Many people, unaware of the real agenda being pursued by the BCSD and of the involvement of Burson-Marsteller, might be inclined to applaud this and celebrate it as a major victory. A closer examination of the document reveals that it glosses over the record of TNCs in creating poverty and environmental destruction. BCSD subscribes to the tenets of neo-classical economic thinking and argues that poverty, not affluence, is the main cause of environmental degradation. In accordance with this philosophy economic growth is essential for sustainable development. The various players have their proper and indispensable roles. Rich countries ought to invest in poor countries and expand trading in every possible way. According to this theory economic growth and trade are the only sure ways to overcome poverty. Poor countries, for their part, ought to dismantle any barriers to foreign investment and open up their markets to foreign goods.

On the second front, the UN General Assembly had instructed the meeting to produce 'specific agreements and commitments by governments for defined activities to deal with major environmental issues'.[7] The corporate sector wanted no such specific agreements. Biotechnological industries in the US prodded the US government not to sign the Treaty on Biodiversity. They balked at the section which called for effective monitoring and enforcement procedures which would benefit Third World and tropical countries. The Treaty on Climate Change was watered down at the insistence of the coal and oil lobby. Any mention of specific targets for the reduction of carbon dioxide emissions or a realistic timeframe was dropped. The BCSD championed voluntary rather than legislated reduction in key pollutants like those found in toxic waste.

Environmental organizations like Greenpeace saw through the smokescreen and dismissed the BCSD initiative as a public relations exercise aimed at diverting any real analysis of the actual causes of environmental degradation and the role of the TNCs in destruction and plunder. In their pamphlet *The Greenpeace Book of Greenwash* they cast a cold eye over the record of many TNCs represented on the BCSD and accused them of cynically jumping on the environment bandwagon, not to protect the environment but to increase sales under a Green banner. Their stinging indictment charged that a leader in ozone destruction takes credit for being a leader in ozone protection; a giant oil company professes to take a 'precautionary approach' to global warming; a major agrochemical manufacturer trades in a pesticide so hazardous that it has been banned in many countries, while implying that the company is helping to feed the hungry. . . . This is 'Greenwash', where TNCs are preserving and expanding their markets by posing as friends of the environment and leaders in the struggle to eradicate poverty. In Paul Hawken's judgement, 'Environment ad campaigns represent the limit and extent to which corporations are presently willing to accept ecological truths'.[8]

THE IMPORTANCE OF ACTION

Only individuals working alone and in groups will effect real change in the ethos and practices of business corporations. One way individuals can challenge the behaviour of TNCs is to boycott their products. One of the most successful boycotts in recent years was mounted against Nestlé, one of the world's leading beverage corporations. Nestlé was challenged to change its practice of aggressively advertising a powder substitute for mothers' milk. This was leading to malnourishment and numerous deaths among infants in Third World countries, especially where water sources were polluted. The campaign was so successful in both the North and South that Nestlé was forced to adopt the UN World Health Organization (WHO) Code of Conduct on baby foods. Unfortunately changes at the UN have allowed Nestlé and TNCs to water down the Code. A renewed boycott was begun in 1989 but it does not have the same momentum as the original one.

The churches must be as vigilant as the development and environment NGOs in challenging TNCs to transform themselves radically. Churches should be able to mobilize their international links to gather accurate information about how particular TNCs are operating. They should also be able to help to support and bring together groups in various countries who are attempting to combat the abuses which a TNC is responsible for in different countries.

One successful example are the communities who are affected by pollution from Union Carbide. This is a coalition of community groups in the US, all of whom are fighting this giant chemical corporation. These groups also have links with the victims of the Bhopal disaster in India.[9] This latter international outreach is extremely important as TNCs faced with stiffening regulations in First World countries are simply moving South to countries which lack environmental legislation or adequate enforcement mechanisms.

At a national level the churches should support legislation that secures workers' rights, controls the power of TNCs to shut down and relocate facilities at will, and protects the environment. They should not allow themselves to be wrong-footed by the disparaging remarks which many corporate spokespersons are presently making against regulations which protect public health and the environment. The churches should also co-operate with others in promoting international legislation to control corporations. One of the more successful treaties was the Montreal Protocol on the Ozone Layer which obliged corporations to phase out the production of CFCs, though they fought the regulations every step of the way.

Given the diminution of political power at the national level which has taken place in recent years, the courts have now become one of the most effective locations in which to combat TNCs. Recently a Texan judge has allowed banana workers in Costa Rica to sue Shell in the United States. The workers claim that they have become sterile as a result of using a particular pesticide. This move means that corporations may be held liable in their country of origin – where environmental and social legislation may be stronger, and compensation and legal costs higher – for activities which they carry out in other countries. Naturally the corporate world is worried and intends to fight this potentially precedent-setting case with all its vast resources.[10]

NEW HOPE

Industry and commerce are not, however, unredeemable acccording to successful businessman, Paul Hawken. In his book *The Ecology of Commerce*, which I have referred to already, he criticizes the economics and ethos of much of contemporary business: 'Quite simply, our business practices are destroying life on earth.'[11] But Hawken does not succumb to a paralysing fatalism that things cannot change. He believes that business can and must mimic nature, where everything is reused and recycled, and that this can make good business sense by lowering costs and retaining customers through the production of superior and more durable goods and better services.

In nature, the waste of one organism becomes the food for another so nothing is lost. Hawken's book sketches a future symbiosis of business, customers and ecology.[12] He claims that such a restorative, sustainable economy could provide more and better jobs, create a more healthy and secure environment, and lead to an overall improvement in the quality of life for people.

To achieve this, Hawken offers some guidelines for sustainable, innovative enterprises. These are not meant to be either exhaustive or to become a potential strait-jacket aimed at stifling creativity. They are simply guidelines, a starting point. Sustainable businesses should:

- Replace nationally and internationally produced items with products created locally or regionally. A community which consumes locally produced goods and services exports less capital and is less likely to deplete or pollute its own environment by either its manufacturing processes or agricultural practices. Hawken quotes Wendell Berry's comment that a restorative company 'finds the shortest, simplest way between the earth, the hands and the mouth'.
- Take responsibility for the effects they have on the natural world. An example of radical redesign which he offers is the work of Sally Fox, the founder of Natural Cotton Colours, Inc. She has bred cotton with a variety of natural colours, thus eliminating the need for toxic dyes and mordants.
- Not require exotic sources of capital in order to grow and develop. Hawken cautions against the dangers of venture capital which can easily become 'vulture' capital. He acknowledges that a number of financial institutions take seriously their responsibility to fund local needs and activities. One such institution is the South Shore Bank in Chicago which, since its inception in 1973, has provided loans for local needs. The Grameen Bank, founded in Bangladesh and now present in many Southern countries, is another such institution which provides the poor with capital for personal and business needs.
- Engage in production processes and services that are humane, worthy, dignified and intrinsically satisfying.
- Create objects of durability and long-term utility whose ultimate use or disposition will not be harmful for future generations.
- Change consumers into customers through education.

Some will say that these and other alternative policies are not practical. They will point out that they are neither economically viable nor politically attainable in the present global climate. I have experienced this kind of response myself, often tinged with condescending smiles, when dealing with officials at government level and in multilateral institutions. The often unspoken reaction is that, while they might sound good in theory, they are based on naïve assumptions and are quite impractical.

At a Third World debt seminar in Tokyo, in November 1992, a colleague of mine, Fr Eugene Ryan, outlined the history of the debt crisis and its impact on the lives of the poor. He made a number of suggestions for both cancelling Third World debts and promoting more people-centred development. The automatic reaction of a Professor of Economics from Sophia University was to say 'If you knew anything about economics, Father, you wouldn't say what you have just said'. Fr Ryan responded by saying that he did know something about economics and that the scenario that he had outlined, in terms of the impact of the debt on the poor, was intolerable from any moral or religious viewpoint. He went on to say that 'If contemporary economic theory supported such gross inequity, then it needed to be speedily and drastically revamped'. A lively discussion ensued. After an hour or so, during which the professor was challenged to face the human and ecological tragedy of contemporary monetarist economic policies, he admitted that – maybe – he needed to take a second look at some of the presuppositions he had accepted so readily.

NOTES

1   Frederic Clairmont and John Cavanagh, 'The rise of the TNC', *Third World Resurgence*, no. 40, pp. 18–20.
2   Quoted in Paul Ekins, Mayer Hillman and Robert Hutchison (eds), *Wealth Beyond Measure* (London: Gaia Books).
3   'The Fortune 500', *Fortune* (20 April 1992).
4   Richard Barnet and John Cavanagh, 'The world the transnationals have built', *Third World Resurgence*, no. 40, p. 21.
5   From the 'Fortune directory of the 500 largest US industrial corporations', *Fortune* (4 May 1982 and 22 April 1991), quoted in *Jobs and the Environment*, private circulation (New York: The Public Health Institute and Labor Institute), p. 146.
6   Nelson Joyce, 'The great global greenwash: Burson-Marsteller vs. the environment', *Third World Resurgence*, no. 37 (September 1993), pp. 5–10.
7   Quoted in André Carothers, 'The green machine', *New Internationalist* (August 1993).
8   Paul Hawken, *The Ecology of Commerce* (New York: HarperCollins, 1993), p. 130.
9   Joshua Karliner, 'Confronting TNCs: some thoughts and strategies', *Third World Resurgence*, no. 40, p. 35.
10   Ibid., p. 36.
11   Paul Hawken, op. cit., p. 3.
12   Ibid., p. 18.

CHAPTER 6

Church response and prophecy

Every individual on earth ought to be challenged to do what s/he can do to halt and reverse the destruction which I have described in the previous chapters. But individual lifestyle changes, however important, will not be sufficient. Real change will only happen when every institution in society – education, health, media, the military, industry, commerce and church – begins to take this message seriously and integrate it into its *modus operandi*. This chapter will look at how the Christian churches, especially the Catholic Church, have responded to this crisis to date and how they might improve their performance and accept a more prophetic role when facing these serious issues.

THE CATHOLIC CHURCH'S LATE ARRIVAL

It is a sad fact of recent history that the churches have been slow to recognize the gravity of the ecological problems facing the earth. They may have felt, like the preacher in the book of Ecclesiastes, that while people and nations have histories the earth is unchanging: 'a generation goes, a generation comes, yet the earth stands firm for ever' (Ecclesiastes 1:4).

Despite the evidence which has been piling up before their eyes church leaders, in common with leaders in the educational, industrial, and financial establishments, have refused to pay attention to what is happening to the delicate fabric of life on earth. Many people might have expected a greater sensitivity to nature from the Catholic Church since the sacraments play such a pivotal role in the life of the Church. Unfortunately, in the aftermath of the Galileo débâcle, the Catholic Church was ill-equipped to dialogue in a creative way with science. In recent centuries the Catholic Church tended to cut itself off from the wider European intellectual ferment which it could no longer control. As a result it relied exclusively on its own heritage in shaping its identity and presenting its message to the world. In the nineteenth century, for example, especially in the era of Pope Pius IX, Church apologetics often portrayed the ideas and proponents of modern science as dangerous enemies of the faith.

While this attitude changed in the twentieth century, it did not lead to a creative, mutually challenging and enriching dialogue. On the one hand the treatment meted out to the Jesuit palaeontologist and theologian Teilhard de Chardin, who was refused permission to publish his works, illustrates that the mutual suspicion between ecclesiastics and scientists is not so easily put to rest. On the other hand church leaders, like many others, were lulled into a false security by some of the successes of modern technology, especially in the area of medicine. They failed to understand both the extent of the despoilment of creation and the urgency with which it must be faced. Unless this awareness is gained quickly and remedial action taken human beings and the rest of the planet's community will be condemned to live amid the ruins of the natural world.

To illustrate this point one needs only to turn to recent Catholic Church teachings. The Second Vatican Council (convened in the 1960s) is, undoubtedly, the major achievement of the Catholic Church in the twentieth century. The Council reconnected the Church to its origins in scripture and helped it find a new identity in itself and face the modern world with confidence and a message of hope. The Council document *Gaudium et Spes* (*The Church in the Modern World*, 1965), is a milestone in the history of the Church's stance towards the world. It embodies a positive, liberating vision of life which refuses to seal off the religious world from the rest of human affairs.

One cannot, however, argue that it is grounded in an ecological vision of reality. This document subscribes to what is called 'dominion theology'. In this perspective the natural world exists primarily for man's exclusive use: 'for man, created in God's image, received a mandate to subject to himself all that it contains, and govern the world with justice and holiness' (no. 34). This anthropocentric bias is even more marked in no. 12 of the same document. It claims almost universal agreement for the teaching that 'according to the unanimous opinion of believers and unbelievers alike, all things on earth should be related to man as their centre and crown'. The cultures of tribal peoples worldwide and of countless Hindus and Buddhists in Asia can hardly be used to bolster up that claim!

Despite Vatican II's mammoth achievement in helping to bring the Catholic Church into the modern world it did not have its ear finely tuned to this vital issue. It did not pick up the growing apprehension which many people shared, even then, about the future of the biosphere. It is worth remembering that Fairfield Osborn's book *Our Plundered Planet* was published in 1948, and Rachel Carson's book *Silent Spring* in April 1962. The Council began in October 1962.

Populorum Progressio (*The Development of Peoples*) appeared in 1967 and was one of the finest documents on the social teaching of the Church to emerge from Rome in the past 30 years. However, it too was insensitive to ecological issues. In its discussion of authentic development the document contained no caution against the impact of industrialization on the biosphere. No. 25 boldly states that 'The introduction of industry is necessary for economic growth and human progress; it is also a sign of development and contributes to it. By persistent work and the use of his intelligence man gradually wrests nature's secrets from her and finds a better application for her riches.' This reflects the hubris of 'man the transformer' which we readily associate with Francis Bacon. It forgets that the greenhouse effect, the depletion of the ozone layer, acid rain, soil erosion, pollution of the seas and rivers, and nuclear waste are a direct result of the Industrial Revolution.

Happily, in the encyclical *Sollicitudo Rei Socialis* (*Social Concerns*), published in 1988, the environment entered into mainline Catholic social teaching. While Catholics can rejoice that this crucial issue has finally found a place on the agenda of the papal magisterium, it is important to remember that by 1988 most institutions and political leaders had already moved or spoken extensively on the ecological crisis. Politicians from as diverse backgrounds as Margaret Thatcher and Eduard Shevardnadze had recognized the issue, and the Brundtland Report, *Our Common Future*, had been published in 1987.[1]

The most important statement in *Sollicitudo Rei Socialis* (SRC) affirmed that humans are living in a limited world and therefore there are physical and moral limits on humans' exploitation of the natural world (no. 34). This supports the questions regarding the appropriate scale of economic activity which I discussed earlier. In no. 37 Pope John Paul II moves beyond the anthropocentric boundaries and challenges those who insist that 'humankind . . . can make arbitrary use of the earth, subjecting it without restraint to the human will, as though it did not have its own requisites and prior God-given purpose, which humankind can develop but not betray'.[2]

On 1 January 1990 Pope John Paul II issued a document for the World Day of Peace celebration, *Peace with God the Creator, Peace with All Creation*. This is the first document from the papal magisterium devoted exclusively to environmental issues. Its main significance is that it calls attention to the moral and religious dimensions of the environmental crisis (nos 2, 7 and 15). In a sentence that will probably come as a surprise to many Catholics the Pope insists that 'Christians, in particular, realize that *their responsibility within creation and their duty towards nature and the Creator are an essential part of their faith*' (emphasis mine). This excellent and unambiguous document is very different from many other church documents and is heavily dependent on the Justice, Peace and the Integrity of Creation (JPIC) programme which the World Council of Churches launched at its Assembly in Vancouver in 1983, though this is not acknowledged in the text.

The Vatican has, unfortunately, been slow to support the World Council of Churches' initiative in the area of Justice, Peace and the Integrity of Creation. Though the European Catholic Bishops' Conference had no problem sponsoring a JPIC Conference in Basel in May 1989, the Vatican refused to accept the invitation to co-sponsor the World Convocation on JPIC which took place in Seoul in 1990. The reason given by the Vatican – that the Catholic Church and the WCC had a different understanding of ecclesial communion – sounds rather lame given the challenges facing the earth and humankind.

Pope John Paul II issued *Centesimus Annus* on 1 May 1991 to mark the 100th anniversary of the first major encyclical on social teaching, *Rerum Novarum*. The document looks back with what some would consider rose-tinted spectacles on the Catholic Church's contribution to social change during the past 100 years.

One full chapter is devoted to the collapse of Marxism and centrally planned economies in Europe in 1989.

No commentator could claim that the environment or questions of sustainable development are central to the text, however they do occur in passing, notably in no. 37. Here the Pope insists that the problem of consumerism is closely related to the ecological issue. Instead of discussing the issue at some depth the Pope moves back to the human agenda in the next paragraph and asserts that 'in addition to the irrational destruction of the natural environment, we must also mention the more serious destruction of the human environment'.

There seems to be very little awareness of the document's heavy dose of domination theology. In no. 43 the Pope looks at new possibilities. He writes that 'In the light of today's "new things", we have to re-read the relationship between individual or private property and the universal destination of material wealth. Man fulfils himself by using his intelligence and freedom. In doing so he utilizes the things of this world as objects and instruments and makes them his own.' The text views the universe as a collection of objects to be transformed, rather than as a communion of subjects. Human work is rigidly set outside the rhythms of the planet's work. There is no attempt to see human work as an activity in continuity with the work of nature, as for example in agriculture. In no. 51 the Pope declares that 'The Church renders this service to human society by preaching the truth about the creation of the world which God has placed in human hands so that people may make it more fruitful and more perfect through their work'. There is little realization that the opposite has in fact happened, and that humans are effectively sterilizing the earth by many of the processes of modern technology.

The inability to see beyond the human agenda also surfaced in the Holy See's submission to the Rio Earth Summit in June 1992. This stated that 'The ultimate purpose of environmental and development programmes is to enhance the quality of human life, *to place creation in the fullest possible way at the service of the human family*' (emphasis mine). Most of the press attention focused on the section of the document which reiterated the position of the Catholic Church on artificial means of birth control. Unfortunately there was little concern about the homocentric theological and philosophical assumptions which underpin the document. These reinforce a world-view which legitimizes human domination of nature.

THE CATECHISM AND CONFERENCE STATEMENTS

The English translation of the new *Catechism of the Catholic Church* finally appeared on Trinity Sunday 1994.[3] Most of the controversy centred not on the content of the book but on the use of sexist language in the final, Vatican-approved version. The Bishops of England and Wales admitted that some readers may feel 'excluded by the style and choice of language' used in the English translation.[4]

Thankfully, the English translation has an excellent index of scriptural texts and a subject index, so it is comparatively easy to evaluate its understanding and treatment of JPIC issues. Most of these are clustered under topics like creation, development, economy and stewardship.

To begin on a positive note, there is some discussion on creation, especially in the section on a 'catechesis on creation' (nos 282 and 378). It affirms that 'because creation comes forth from God's goodness, it shares in that goodness', and goes on to state that 'On many occasions the Church has had to defend the goodness of creation, including that of the physical world' (no. 299). While 'each creature possesses its own particular goodness and dignity' (no. 339), 'man is at the summit of the Creator's work' (no. 343). Nevertheless, 'There is a solidarity among all creatures arising from the fact that all have the same Creator and are all ordered to his glory' (no. 344).

In its discussion of the seventh commandment the catechism urges respect for the integrity of creation:

> Animals, like plants and inanimate beings, are by nature destined for the common good of past, present and future humanity. Use of the mineral, vegetable and animal resources of the universe cannot be divorced from respect for moral imperatives. Man's dominion over inanimate and other living beings granted by the Creator is not absolute; it is limited by concern for the quality of life of his neighbour, including generations to come; it requires a religious respect for the integrity of creation. (no. 2415)

Although the catechism does deal with JPIC issues it touches on them in a rather light and sparing manner: a few pages out of the total 610. The themes are not a central concern of the catechism. There is very little recognition of the magnitude and urgency of either the cry of the poor or the cry of the earth. The evil of Third

World debt is not highlighted, for example, in the section on 'The Social Doctrine of the Church' (nos 2419–49). The possibility of a link between liturgy and creation as a way of developing an ecological catechesis is never raised. Nor does the present devastation of the natural world figure in the discussion of the sacraments. Though Original Sin breaks the harmony between humans and creation (no. 400), there is no thought of reconciliation with nature as a fruit of the sacrament of penance.

The presentation on the fifth commandment includes areas like war, abortion, homicide, suicide and euthanasia. However the extinction of species or biocide is not mentioned. For Fr Tom Berry this is one of the major sins of this generation. He is appalled that Christians are unaware of the grim reality of extinction. For him the extinction of species has an urgency and poignancy because of its eternal consequences. He writes:

> Extinction is an eternal concept. It is not at all like the killing of an individual life form that can be renewed by the normal processes of reproduction . . . nor is it something that can be remedied . . . nor is it something which affects only our own generation . . . No! it is an absolute and final act for which there is no remedy on earth or in heaven.[5]

Given what is at stake – nothing less than the future well-being of the planet – the catechism should have spelled out more clearly the responsibility of individual Christians and churches towards the poor of the earth and creation itself. A golden opportunity has been lost to spotlight the reality of ecological sin and thereby educate Catholics about what is happening to the earth today and what the implications are for this and future generations. Nicholas Lash captures this kind of urgency when he writes that 'Those who destroy the beauty of creation or who create ugliness may be sinning against the Holy Spirit, God's self-gift in beauty and delight'.[6]

A number of Bishops' Conferences have also issued statements about the environment in their countries. One of the first statements, *What Is Happening to our Beautiful Land?*, came from the Philippines. Bishop James Malone of Youngstown, Ohio, in a talk at Ohio State University in February 1993, said that 'The bishops of the Philippines, in an eloquently worded pastoral letter, took an early lead among the bishops of the world in condemning the devastation of the tropical forests in their country'.[7] In contrast to the catechism and some of the previous church texts this document does recognize the gravity of the devastation. In the opening paragraph it states: 'Our country is in peril. All the living systems on land and in the seas around us are being ruthlessly exploited. The damage to date is extensive and, sad to say, is often irreversible.'[8]

OTHER CHRISTIAN CHURCHES

In this book I restrict my attention to the place of justice, peace and the integrity of creation within the Catholic Church. It is nevertheless important to recognize the important work which the World Council of Churches has done under the aegis of its Justice, Peace and the Integrity of Creation programme.[9] As I pointed out on page 106 above, this influenced Pope John Paul II's *Peace with God the Creator, Peace with All Creation*. Still, it must be acknowledged that the Catholic Church is not the only Christian church that has failed in protecting creation because of its overly human-centred theological perspective. The churches of the Reformation highlighted the importance of the scriptures and justification by faith. The quest for salvation was centred on the individual human person, an understandable reaction against the corporatism of the time. Unfortunately it glorified individualism and further intensified the dualism between the spiritual and worldly kingdom. The Irish Methodist theologian Johnston McMaster believes that 'The location of God's Kingdom in the soul eliminated God from the ecological as well as the political arena.'[10] In this tradition the earth is there to be used by humankind and whatever is not of use to humankind has no value in itself.

Even the Methodist tradition, nurtured on the hymns of Charles Wesley, is excessively personal and forgetful of the wider earth and cosmic context. Wesley's hymns celebrate the universality of grace, but always within a human context. The creation and cosmic dimensions of theology and spirituality are more or less absent. McMaster holds that modern Methodists have not yet developed a theology of universal grace beyond the anthropocentric. 'Nor have they developed the oft-quoted slogan from John Wesley "friends of all and enemies of none", politically or ecologically. What might it mean, in relation to animate and inanimate creation, to affirm that we are friends of all and enemies of none?'[11]

ACKNOWLEDGING THE PROBLEM

What is the most important contribution which religious institutions like the churches can make in response to the present ecological crisis? The primary challenge to the churches, which they have failed to face in any significant way thus far, is to remind people at all times of the magnitude of the crisis and the urgency with which it must be faced. This concern is central to the WCC's JPIC programme.

Much of the data on the deteriorating state of our air, water, soils and tropical forests is now generally accepted as accurate by the scientific community. In November 1992 over 1,500 scientists, including many Nobel prize-winners, issued a statement in which they said that human beings and the natural world are on a collision course: 'No more than one or a few decades remain before the chance to avoid the threats we now confront will be lost.'[12]

This knowledge is not new. Almost a decade and a half ago it appeared in the *Global 2000 Report to the President*. This report, which was published in 1980 and addressed to US President Carter, was one of the first comprehensive attempts to document the environmental devastation which has taken place in recent decades. The letter of transmission read: 'If present trends continue, the world in 2000 will be more crowded, more polluted, less ecologically stable and more vulnerable to disruption than the world we live in now.'[13]

One major consequence of the destruction of the tropical rainforests, the most diverse ecosystem on earth, is the rapid acceleration of species extinction in recent decades. To date almost 55 per cent of the total rainforest area worldwide has been destroyed. As we saw earlier the Harvard biologist E. O. Wilson, who has engaged in extensive field-work in Amazonia, is so alarmed at the rate of extinction that he insists that 'ruling out nuclear war, the worst thing now taking place is the loss of genetic diversity'.[14] His anxiety is shared by scores of biologists in both the South and the North. In the Philippines, for example, botanists and biologists assumed that 33 per cent of species were endemic. Seeing that two-thirds of the forests has already been destroyed it is fair to assume that the rate of extinction in recent decades has been enormous. A USAID report published in 1989 confirms this and estimates that over half the species which are unique to the Philippines have already been driven to extinction.[15]

A number of authors attempted to refute the arguments put forward in *Global 2000*. In *The Resourceful Earth* Julian Simon and Herman Kahn of the Hudson Institute dismissed the concerns of ecologists and questioned the assumptions, statistical data and perspective of *Global 2000*.[16] In a parody of the letter of transmission they predicted that 'If present trends continue, the world in 2000 will be less crowded (though more populated), less polluted, more stable ecologically and less vulnerable to resource supply disruption than the world we live in now.'[17] Fourteen years later, with a spate of new, worrying data being published on every aspect of the environment, it is clear that the perspective of *Global 2000* is much closer than was that of Simon and Kahn.

And yet Julian Simon is still dismissing data on environmental devastation and disparaging environmentalists. In a 1993 article, 'So biodiversity is doomed?', Simon and his co-writer Wildavsky are not convinced by arguments at either the macro or the micro level. Both these authors refuse to look at the larger picture.[18] Since a huge portion of the rainforests has already been destroyed it is logical, given the interdependent nature of ecosystems, to deduce that an unacceptably high number of species have been driven to extinction. For those concerned about passing on a fruitful earth to the next generation the most pressing task is twofold: firstly, it is necessary to discover the causes for environmental destruction and, secondly, to change the economic and political policies which are responsible. Instead of taking this tack, Simon and Wildavsky blame the messenger. The villain of the piece, according to them, is the British biologist Norman Myers, whose book *The Sinking Ark* was one of the first texts to focus attention on the extinction of species.

Simon and Wildavsky accuse Myers of misusing data and of a flawed analysis. They, however, fail to paint an adequate picture of the astonishing species and genetic diversity which are found in rainforests. Furthermore they base their claim, that there is no need for alarm since only minimal rates of extinction have occurred, on extrapolating from data gathered in temperate forests in North America. This, of course, is not comparing like with like! Reflecting on the enormous diversity traditionally found in the Philippines, the USAID study estimated that 'there were more wood plant species at Mt Makiling [a mountain on the island of Luzon] than in the whole continental United States'.[19]

Faced with the overwhelming evidence of environmental devastation the most seductive approach for those not disposed to action is *not* to follow Simon and Kahn and deny that anything disastrous is taking place. Almost everyone has experienced some environmental problem; so the public would be sceptical of anyone who would simply deny that there is a problem. The more insidious tactic is to downplay the crisis and question the scientific basis on which some of the data is based. While doubts are being systematically cultivated governments or corporations can postpone installing safeguards, especially if they are costly, and justify their behaviour by the lack of scientific clarity. In an atmosphere of doubt and confusion industry and regulators will not be compelled to take any remedial action, especially if such actions might appear to undermine Northern affluence, lower corporate profits or threaten jobs.

A typical example of this tactic is the case of DuPont and the handling of the CFCs debate. A *Time* magazine (10 May 1993), article 'Who lost the ozone?' revealed the saga of confusion, indecision, incompetence and duplicity on the part of the corporation and government officials who worked with each other to protect corporate profits rather than the common good. DuPont, the largest producer of ozone-depleting CFCs, argued as late as the 1980s that CFCs were short-lived and therefore not a long-term threat to the environment (despite ample proof since the late 1970s that this was incorrect). In addition, to avoid any Congressional legislation that might adversely affect them, DuPont sponsored an alliance of CFC users to lobby politicians at their local bases across the US to stave off any regulations on CFC production.

In the *Time* article one of the US government regulators, Robert Watson, accused DuPont of lying about the size of the CFC market during the 1980s. DuPont consistently argued that the market was mature when, in fact, they knew it was growing. The final twist in the saga came in 1986 when DuPont reversed their position on CFCs. At this point they knew that they were ahead of their competitors in research into the production of CFC substitutes and therefore were well placed to reap huge profits.

Politicians, especially, during the Reagan administration, used scientific uncertainty to justify not taking any action to counter the threat. The *Time* article quoted Anne Burford, who was in charge of the EPA in the early Reagan years. She disliked international agreements and 'regarded ozone depletion as an unsubstantiated scare story'. Against a background of such incompetence and bias companies like DuPont took the hint and tailored their research and production accordingly.

The corporate world has a major stake in keeping the status quo in place and it will use any ploy to stall effective action which might undermine its markets and profits. Governments act in this way, too. The US and Britain misused scientific data on the effects of acid rain in order to avoid restrictions on emissions in the energy and transport sectors during the Reagan and Thatcher era. US Vice-President Albert Gore in *The Earth in Balance* illustrates this approach. He points to a leaked document from the Bush administration to White House spokespeople, during the run-up to the Earth Day celebrations for 1990, which directed officials not to deny that global warming was a problem. They were encouraged instead to focus on the many uncertainties in the domain of global warming research to forestall a groundswell of opinion which might insist on effective curbs on the use of fossil fuels and on CO_2 emissions.

WITNESS AND PROPHECY

In the light of efforts to downplay these serious challenges facing humanity, the churches must be resolute in their determination to witness to the truth. There are many pressures, both inside and outside the churches, to encourage them to minimize or evade the issues. They can do this by focusing on other topics or by investing collective energy in more spiritual questions or in the internal affairs of the church. Yet on a number of occasions in recent years Pope John Paul II has drawn attention to the present scale of environmental destruction. For example, after a summer holiday in the Italian Dolomite mountains he warned about the need to protect and rediscover nature in the face of an 'environmental holocaust'.[20] Churches should join in the different campaigns which are attempting to challenge powerful Pharaoh-like institutions. While it is crucial that church people are familiar with the economic and ecological issues involved, the churches must take their stands primarily on moral and religious grounds.

The churches must take a prophetic stance for justice and the integrity of God's creation. There are two complementary elements in the prophetic witness. The first is to criticize the present unjust economic, political and social system which impoverishes people and destroys the environment. The churches must be fearless in their willingness to expose evil and name the sin by refusing to pander to vested interests, no matter what the consequences for the Church as an institution. It would be a betrayal of the Gospel to tone down justice and peace statements in order to promote the churches' institutional well-being. The second dimension of the prophetic witness is often more difficult but it is even more essential. The Church must try to empower people to formulate a new vision of a more equitable and sustainable world. I will discuss this in more detail later.

Politicians often reject the Church's prophetic ministry as meddling in politics which, in their view, should be beyond the pale of religion. In the 1980s the Church of England published *Faith in the City* which highlighted the growing poverty and alienation in cities across Britain. Instead of listening to the cry of the poor many Conservative politicians attempted to discredit the authors of the document. It was easier to blame the messenger than face up to the harsh realities created by their economic policies.

Given the gravity of ecological and justice questions the Church must address these with a sense of urgency and passion. This is not an easy task, however, especially in Northern countries. Even though the living standard of the middle class has been undermined in recent years, and environmental degradation is of concern to many people, the culture of contentment is still very much in place. This culture effectively side-tracks any attempt to advance the radical change of behaviour which will be necessary to promote justice and protect the environment. And yet the churches must embrace this challenge.

The churches' commitment to prophecy springs primarily from two sources. Firstly, it is grounded on faithfulness to the Exodus tradition of liberation and freedom. In this tradition all people are called to freedom and to be daughters and sons of God. Secondly, prophecy arises from the contemporary challenges, both local and global.

Anyone with even a modest familiarity with the scriptures will be aware that Yahweh, the God of Israel, is portrayed as a God of justice and compassion. The covenant faith of Israel emerged out of the experience of oppression and slavery in Egypt, followed by the freedom gained through the Exodus. Consequently, the God of Israel is not portrayed as a guarantor of a stable political, social and economic order, particularly one which is unjust. On the contrary, the God of Israel is experienced as one who strengthens, sustains and assists the oppressed, the marginalized, the weak, the strangers and the debtors in their unequal struggles against their oppressors (Exodus 3:7–12). This God, who is encountered as sovereignly free and therefore not susceptible to manipulation from the rich and powerful, actively confronts the political power of the Pharaoh and the religious ideology which is used to support and underpin that oppressive regime.

The prophets, as the spokespersons of the God of Israel, also confront the rich and powerful within the community of Israel. They do this in concrete situations when the political and religious leaders abandon a concern for all the members of the community, merely serving the interests of the few. In such a situation the prophet is expected to tell things as they really are and not allow facile explanations to mask the true injustice of what is happening. In the contemporary context, the prophet might be expected to cut through the jargon that has surrounded Third World debt and challenge the various mechanisms which have given rise to such pain and destruction.

Not every tradition will allow the cries and criticisms of the underclass to be heard and incorporated into its ethical self-understanding. Other cultures in the ancient world often favoured the rights of property over the rights of people. There are clear indications of this in the famous axiom on rights to property in Roman law – *jus utendi, jus fruendi, jus abutendi* – the right to use, enjoy and abuse. No such rights are conceded in the Hebrew or Christian traditions. These traditions recognize the rights of the poor, the debtors, the widow, the orphans, the defenceless; even the land has rights to its Sabbath rest.

People with property are restricted through a variety of prescriptions from benefiting exclusively from the usufruct of their property. In fact, the possession of property established an obligation on the owner to use that property astutely so that it might benefit the poor, the sojourner and the marginalized. Because they lacked property it was presumed that they would not be able to meet their own basic needs; so it was incumbent on those with possessions to help these people to live with dignity. This outlook is expressed in the Exodus text which follows immediately after the covenant experience of Israel at Sinai:

> You must not molest the stranger or oppress him, for you lived as strangers in the land of Egypt. You must not be harsh to widows, or with the orphan; if you are harsh with them, they will surely cry to me, and be sure I shall hear their cry; my anger will flare and I shall kill you with the sword, your own wives will be widows, your own children orphans. (22:21–24)

The text goes on to prohibit the taking of interest, because it was seen as a sure way of trapping the poor on the treadmill of endless debt:

> If you lend money to any of my people, to any poor man among you, you must not play the usurer with him; you must not demand interest from him. (22:25)

The statistics and case studies which I have quoted throughout this book illustrate how the poor today are being destroyed by the policies of financial institutions. Most Africans are poorer in 1994 than they were in the 1960s since debt servicing siphons off $160 billion annually. This figure is in excess of one-quarter of Africa's export earnings. It is a scandal, in the biblical sense of that word, that the IMF alone has transferred more than $3 billion out of Africa since the mid-1980s without an outcry from the churches.[21]

What has happened in much of the Third World in recent decades is akin to the plunder which the Hebrew scriptures condemned and the prophets like Amos and Joel railed against. In Jamaica, for example, Christian Aid reckons that every individual Jamaican owes Northern commercial banks, governments or multilateral lending agencies almost $1,500. Between 1982 and 1990 Jamaica paid $4.2 billion servicing their debt. However, because of high interest rates and the fall in commodity prices the debt increased by 55 per cent. The majority of Jamaicans are forced to survive on less than $5,000 a year.

Faced with comparable situations the biblical authors did not withdraw into complicated, abstract economic arguments about the evils of usury. The Bible is very direct and concrete. In the following example it recognizes that if something as important as a person's coat is taken as a pledge on a debt, then that garment should be returned before nightfall, otherwise a person might have to sleep without the garment on a cold night and endanger his health or even his very life:

> If you take another's cloak as a pledge, you must give it back to him before sunset. It is all the covering he has; it is the cloak he wraps his body in; what else would he sleep in? If he cries to me, I will listen, for I am full of pity. (Exodus 22:26–27)

Deuteronomy 24 goes even further and forbids a creditor from acting haughtily and storming into a person's house to recover a pledge. The creditor is expected to wait outside the house and allow the debtor to bring out his pledge to him. In the biblical perspective a creditor rushing into a house would constitute an offence to the personal dignity of the debtor. In a covenant community, which promises equality and sharing, this is seen to be oppressive and immoral:

> If you are making your fellow a loan on a pledge, you are not to go into his house and seize the pledge, whatever it may be. You must stay outside, and the man to whom you are making the loan shall bring the pledge to you. (24:10–11).

The same chapter also forbids commandeering the means of livelihood of a person as collateral for a debt. The author understands very well that in an agricultural society if a creditor takes a mill or even the top stone, the debtor is deprived of his livelihood. In certain circumstances, without his millstone, he may well be unable to secure basic food that he and his family need to survive:

> No man may take a mill or a millstone in pledge; that would be to take life itself in pledge. (24:6)

The deluge of criticism of SAPs contained in the 1989 UNICEF report, Marcus Arruda's paper on SAPs in Somalia and the Oxfam report, and countless other aid agencies and missionaries confirm that SAPs have bred illiteracy, malnutrition, starvation, disintegration of economies and death in Africa, Latin America and Southeast Asia. In the language of the Bible they have taken the lives of millions in pledge.

The parallels between what is happening in the Third World today and what Deuteronomy condemns in the domain of debt are so striking that Christian leaders should see it as their duty to condemn it. Though statements have been issued by a number of Episcopal conferences, by the World Council of Churches (WCC) and by the Vatican and Catholic bishops, very few people, including even well-informed Christians, would consider that action in this regard is high on the churches' agenda.

What a difference between the present indifference of Christians and their leaders and the prophets of Israel! In Micah's famous summary of how to live in harmony with the Law acting justly came first:

> This is what Yahweh asks of you, only this:
> to act justly, to love tenderly
> and to walk humbly with your God.
> (Micah 6:8)

Like any other prophet, Micah was not speaking in the abstract and deducing general moral and religious principles. He was giving voice to the protests of the poor country people in his own region of Judea. In eighth-century Judea poor peasants felt the yoke of increased taxes weighing them down. These taxes were being demanded by the political leadership in Jerusalem to finance a burgeoning state apparatus and increase military spending. These policies benefited the urban élite and crippled the poor (Micah 2:1–2; 3:1–2). The situation which Micah addressed so strikingly has clear parallels in modern times, especially with the Third World debt.

A prophetic ministry dispels any illusion that the present inequitable situation is acceptable. The prophet speaks the truth about the shape and extent of the problem. S/he does this in the name of those who have no voice in society. In the light of the equality inherent in the covenant faith of Israel s/he challenges society to face up to what is really happening in its communities. This means exposing the mechanisms whereby communities prefer to forget or deny the oppression and alienation which is deeply rooted in their consciousness. This unwrapping of reality, so that its true contours can be seen, is often best performed through the creative use of language and symbols. It enables communities to cut through the present malaise and find a 'way in which the cover-up and stonewalling can be ended'.[22]

IMAGINING NEW WAYS

Prophecy is a coin with a double image. The prophetic challenge in Israel, for example, was not confined to criticizing and condemning unjust social and political structures.[23] It was also aimed at liberating the imagination to equip people to think new thoughts and envisage new ways of acting in order to cement bonds of solidarity and intimacy between members of the community. Micah holds out that hope:

In the days to come
the mountain of the Temple of Yahweh
will be put on top of the mountains
and be lifted up higher than the hills . . .

(4:1)

He will wield authority over many peoples
and arbitrate for mighty nations;
they will hammer their swords into ploughshares,
and their spears into sickles.   (4:3)

Every man will sit under his vine and fig tree,
with no one to trouble him.

(4:4)

Such new dreams and visions inevitably destroy the 'mythical legitimacy' of the present, exploitative social reality. For this reason the prophet is not a welcomed guest at the tables of those who benefit from the status quo. Moses, a pivotal figure in the prophetic tradition, through his creative leadership and actions, 'dismantled the politics of oppression and exploitation by countering it with the politics of justice and compassion'.[24]

The power to envisage a new way of living when everything is so staid and settled is rooted in a radically new vision of a God who takes sides in human affairs. In the Jewish tradition Yahweh is a God who hears the cry of the poor and supports their concerns. Yahweh has his special interests: the poor and those who live on the margins. The role of the gods of Egypt and the divine in many other societies in the Middle East at the time, however, was to legitimize the political and social pyramid and promote the interests of 'haves', often against the 'have nots'. These gods 'cast their votes' to preserve the political, social and economic status quo for ever.[25]

Similarly today, the search for life-enhancing alternatives creates a variety of challenges. In the area of Third World debt and appropriate development policies it will mean discarding much of the ideology of monetarist economic theory that has inspired the SAPs which have been forced on many Third World countries. A new shape for sustainable economic policies has been suggested by many commentators. Kevin Watkins of Oxfam argues that what Africa needs today are well-designed policies that promote a relaxation of interest rates and support targeted investment in small-scale industries.[26] I would add that well-designed agricultural policies focused on food production rather than export crops and a package of measures to initiate and give momentum to sustainable development are also essential.

Walter Brueggemann argues in *The Prophetic Imagination* that today the consciousness and imagination of many Christians have been co-opted by the dominant economic and political systems. According to him we have been so conditioned by the organs of the Establishment to think in a certain way that we are unable to think any other thoughts. In the area of military spending, for example, political leaders expect people to be silent in the face of the human cost of war and the colossal waste of resources in the armaments industry. The same is true of other areas of national and global economic life which are often controlled by a small élite. They expect people to be blind to the rapacious actions which breed such poverty and environmental destruction. In such a situation, when so many people are cowed into silence, a prophetic ministry is desperately needed. This ought to embolden people to ask 'not whether something is practical or viable, but whether it is *imaginable*. . . . It is the vocation of the prophet to keep alive the ministry of the imagination, to keep conjuring and proposing alternative futures to the single one the king wants to urge as the only thinkable one.'[27]

The Church must attempt to become an alternative community where new visions can be fashioned and new beginnings launched. Such new stirrings are taking place among the poor, the dispossessed and those who are marginalized or directly oppressed by the present order. The Church must become more closely aligned with these communities. In this way it would embody the hopes of many people and could live up to its image of being 'a sign raised up among the nations'. As a faith-filled community it could be bold, imaginative and radical. Such a community could enter more fully into the spirit of Mary's Magnificat and confidently celebrate the power of the One who empowers those who work for justice:

> He has shown the power of his arm,
> he has routed the proud of heart.
> He has pulled down princes from their thrones and exalted the
>   lowly.
> The hungry he has filled with good things, and the rich sent empty
>   away.
>
> (Luke 1:51–53)

Finally, such a community should be committed to walk in the footsteps of Jesus and actively intervene on behalf of the exploited. In his life his word provided hope, and his actions of feeding, healing, forgiving and freeing people from demons and caring for the weak fleshed out that hope. It was out of such a hope-filled context that resurrection could burst forth. This resurrection could become real for millions of people today.

NOTES

1   *Our Common Future: The World Commission on Environment and Development* (Oxford: Oxford University Press, 1987).
2   Quoted in Denis Edward, 'Integrity of creation: Catholic social teaching for an ecological age', *Pacifica*, vol. 5, no. 2 (June 1992), pp. 183–203.
3   *Catechism of the Catholic Church* (London: Geoffrey Chapman, 1994).
4   'Home news', *The Tablet* (23 April 1994), p. 504.
5   Thomas Berry, *Riverdale Papers*, vol. 8 (Riverdale, NY: Riverdale Center for Religious Studies).
6   Quoted in Edward P. Echlin, 'Dare ecology use the word "sin"?', *The Month* (May 1993).
7   Bishop James Malone, 'Environmental degradation and social justice', *Origins*, CNS documentary service (18 March 1993), p. 687.
8   Quoted in Sean McDonagh, *The Greening of the Church* (London: Geoffrey Chapman/Maryknoll, NY: Orbis Books, 1990), Appendix 2.
9   David Gosling, *A New Earth: Covenanting for Justice, Peace and the Integrity of Creation* (London: CCBI (Inter-Church House, 35–41 Lower Marsh, London SE1 7RL), 1992).
10 Johnston McMaster, 'The Church and the environment', unpublished talk given at Queen's University, Belfast (December 1993).
11 Ibid.
12 Quoted in Edward P. Echlin, op. cit.
13 *Global 2000 Report to the President* (Harmondsworth: The Council on Environmental Quality and the Department of Energy, 1980).
14 E. O. Wilson, *Biophilia* (Cambridge, MA: Harvard University Press, 1984), p. 122.
15 International Inc./Institute of Development Anthropology, *Sustainable Natural Resource Assessment – Philippines* (Manila: USAID, 1989).
16 Julian Simon and Herman Kahn, *The Resourceful Earth* (Oxford: Blackwell, 1984).
17 Quoted in Edward Goldsmith and Nicholas Hildyard (eds), *The Earth Report* (London: Mitchell Beazley, 1988), p. 156.
18 Julian Simon and Aaron Wildavsky, 'So biodiversity is doomed? Let's take a cool recount', *International Herald Tribune* (14 May 1993).
19 *Sustainable Natural Resource Assessment – Philippines*, op. cit., p. 15.
20 Quoted in *The Universe* (18 July 1993).
21 Kevin Watkins, 'Theology of the saps threatens poorest of the poor', *Guardian* (10 January 1994).
22 Walter Brueggemann, *The Prophetic Imagination* (Minneapolis: Fortress Press, 1978), p. 49.

23 Ibid., p. 13.
24 Ibid., p. 16.
25 Ibid., p. 24.
26 Kevin Watkins, op. cit.
27 Walter Brueggemann, op. cit., p. 44.

CHAPTER 7

Eco-centred ethics and
Christian hope

THE CHOICES WHICH PEOPLE MAKE in their daily lives spring from the values which society espouses. For this reason it is worth reflecting on the values which drive our global economy. Most commentators would maintain that economic considerations are the main impetus behind the saga of destruction today. Neo-classical economists might argue that economics, like other sciences, is value-free. In reality, economies, whether local or simple or global and complex, are driven by the values which humans consider to be desirable. It is essential to lay bare the dysfunctional values which underpin our present economic system, before one can confront them and substitute other values. The Church should challenge our earth-consuming culture and unmask the contemporary idols which are seducing many people and fostering untold pain, exploitation and destruction.

Unfortunately it is not always true that 'religious' values are always life-giving and that it is secular values which are problematic. Religious people often subscribe to this misconception, as did the Vatican document submitted to the Rio Summit. It assumed that religious values will act as an antidote to earth-destroying values. This, of course, is not always the case. Some of the values which I will identify as contributing to the destruction of the earth have roots in our Christian religious heritage. So the Church, along with other institutions, must also strike its breast and pursue the path of conversion. In the process it can begin to fashion a theology which will address the new challenges in an effective way, discover new insights into the scriptures and realize a new urgency for its message of love and hope in the contemporary world.

ANTHROPOCENTRISM – THE HUMAN-CENTRED AGENDA

Almost every aspect of Western culture, from religion to science, is extremely anthropocentric. In our modern world this human-centred hubris is most clearly seen in the areas of Western science and technology. These are seen as providing humans with power over the natural world which, in turn, is seen as raw material to be manipulated and moulded by humans for their own purposes and betterment. The writings of Francis Bacon, René Descartes and Isaac Newton provided the intellectual justification for the progressive drive to manipulate and conquer nature. However, anthropocentrism has a much longer ancestry. Its roots go deep into the earliest forms of Western consciousness in both the Jewish and Greek experience.

Human-centredness, with its concomitant dualism of body/spirit and male/female and its hierarchical method of valuing reality, is pervasive and has numerous manifestations. It also colours a person's understanding of the reality and role of the Divine. God is most often seen as sovereign and superior to nature, occupying the top rung of the ladder of Being and possessing male attributes. As Pierre Gassendi (one of the founders of the French Academy of Sciences) put it in the seventeenth century: 'God is not the soul of the world, but its governor and director.'[1]

The will to dominate the earth begins with an understanding that humans are radically different from everything else in creation. It assumes that there is an unbridgeable chasm between humans and the rest of creation. Humans alone are endowed with spirit. They are unique in so far as they are created in 'the image and likeness of God' (Genesis 1:26). This likeness (*imago Dei*) is seen primarily in their spiritual faculties, like intelligence and will. Humans are seen as superior to the rest of creation and in some ways not an integral part of it. We think we have more affinity with spiritual beings, like angels, than with the rest of the animal world. Psalm 8:5 reflects this in its jubilant cry: 'You have made him little less than a god.'

The rest of creation is perceived as not having any sacred dimension. It is simply matter, consequently not prized or valued.

Its primary purpose is to be a resource base in order to meet human needs. The historian Keith Thomas writes in *Man and the Natural World* that during the sixteenth and seventeenth centuries Western literature, theology and popular preaching ascribed no intrinsic value to the natural world. With the natural world shorn of any religious values and inherent rights the Genesis command, 'Be fruitful, multiply, fill the earth and conquer it. Be masters of the fish of the sea, the birds of the heaven and all the living animals on the earth' (1:28), could easily be invoked to legitimize any human exploitation of the natural world.[2] Clive Ponting concurs with this view in *A Green History of the World*. Looking at the broad sweep of European culture he finds that

A strong conviction running through both classical and Christian tradition has been that human beings have been put in a position of dominance over the rest of a subordinate nature. Although the ideas that humans have a responsibility to preserve a natural world of which they are merely guardians can be traced through a succession of thinkers, it has remained a minority tradition.[3]

In the seventeenth century thinkers like René Descartes and Francis Bacon added their voices to this human-centred chorus. As founding fathers of modern science they recognized that the emerging scientific revolution would give humans greater control over nature. For Bacon the scientific venture, which consisted of understanding nature in order to regulate it more effectively, took on the overtones of a religious vocation or crusade. Once rebellious nature was tamed the complete human control which was thought to have existed in Paradise before the Fall would be restored. Thus, in Descartes' celebrated phrase, it would make humans 'masters and possessors of nature'.

For Ponting and Thomas modern European attitudes towards nature spring from both the Greco-Roman and the Jewish heritage. The American historian Lynn White, in his now famous lecture delivered at the American Association for the Advancement of Science in 1966, narrows the field of blame and concentrates on the religious roots of Western culture. He indicts the Christian tradition and maintains that our present ecological troubles will continue until there is a major shift in Westerners' religious perspective.

White maintains that Westerners feel 'superior to nature, contemptuous of it, and willing to use it for our slightest whim'.[4]

Many theologians and scripture scholars point out that this view of nature is not an accurate interpretation of the Genesis text. Ted F. Peters is adamant that the command cannot be interpreted as a licence for humans to change and transform the natural world according to any human whim or fantasy. The command, in fact, is a challenge to humans to imitate God's loving kindness and faithfulness and to act as his/her viceroys in relationship with the non-human components of the earth community. This, he argues, is the original meaning of the Hebrew word *radah* used in the text. Like viceroys of the king, men and women are expected to be just, honest, and render real service.[5]

While all this may well be true, the domination perspective is still a generally accepted reading of the first account of creation in Genesis 1:1 – 2:4 for many Christians today. This places humans on top of a pyramid in which those above have the right to exploit those lower down. In his essay 'Saving nature, but only for man' in *Time* (17 June 1991) Charles Krauthammer presents a modern, secular articulation of the domination perspective: 'I like caribou as much as the next man. And I would be rather sorry if their mating patterns are disturbed. But you can't have everything. And if the choice is between the welfare of the caribou and reducing oil dependency that gets people killed in wars, I choose man over caribou every time.'

In discussing the appropriate scale for human activity on the planet, the economist Herman Daly contrasts what he calls an 'empty world' and a 'full world'.[6] The 'empty world' refers to the impact which a small population of human beings with limited technology made on the biosphere in the past. The 'full world' refers to the extraordinary impact which contemporary humans with their powerful technologies make on the rest of creation. In the 'empty world' it might have been possible to respect the rights of other creatures while meeting expanding human needs. But in the crowded world of today, where humans are appropriating more and more of the creatures and goods of the planet for their exclusive use, that luxury is quickly disappearing.

Unless we develop clear moral principles to guide our behaviour towards other creatures there is little possibility that many will survive. Krauthammer is in no doubt about his answer to the question: How can human rights and the rights of nature be reconciled?

The important distinction is between those environmental
goods that are fundamental and those that are merely
aesthetic. Nature is our ward. It is not our master. It is to be
respected and even cultivated. But it is a man's world. When
man has to choose between his well-being and that of nature,
nature will have to accommodate.

It is worth noting that Krauthammer's assertion that 'it is a man's
world' is literally correct. The anthropocentric (man at the centre)
world-view leads to relationships of domination over nature,
women, people of colour and the poor.

The need to repent, abandon anthropocentrism and choose a life-
centred ethic was very much to the fore in the celebrated address by
the Korean theologian Chung Hyun-Kyung at the 1991 World
Council of Churches (WCC) meeting in Canberra.

One of the most crucial agendas for our generation is to learn
how to live with the earth, promoting harmony, sustainability
and diversity. Traditional Christian creation theology and
Western thinking puts the human, especially men, at the
centre of the created world and men have had the power to
control and dominate the creation. Modern science and
development models are based on this assumption. We should
remember, however, that this kind of thinking is alien to many
Asian people and the indigenous people of the world. For us
the earth is the source of life and nature is 'sacred, purposeful
and full of meaning'. Human beings are a very small part of
nature, not above it. For example, for Filipinos the earth is
their mother. They call her *Ina*. *Ina* means 'mother' in
Tagalog. *Ina* is the great goddess from whom all life comes. As
you respect your mother, you should respect the earth. Isn't it
true also that in the Christian tradition we affirm that we all
come from the earth? God made us from the dust of the
earth.[7]

STEWARDSHIP

To return to the biblical texts: scholars maintain that the second
account of creation, Genesis 2:4 – 3:24, is much older and much
more earthy than the account in Genesis 1. In this cluster of stories
humans are created by Yahweh from the earth, *'adamah*, a play on

the word *'adam*. 'Yahweh God fashioned man of dust from the soil. Then he breathed into his nostrils a breath of life, and thus man became a living being' (2:7). The image used here is that of the master potter carefully moulding the clay until a beautiful piece of pottery emerges. Yet even here the most crucial factor in human emergence, the breath of life, is not derived from the earth but from the breath of Yahweh.

In this account Yahweh's involvement with humans does not end with the act of creation. Yahweh planted a garden for humans and 'took man and put him in the garden of Eden to till it and keep it' (2:15). The Hebrew words used here are *abad* and *shamar*. *Abad* means to 'work' or 'till' but it also has overtones of service, while *shamar* means 'keep' with overtones of preserving and defending from harm. This verse is often used to champion the notion of stewardship as one of the most appropriate Judeo-Christian concepts for addressing the environmental question. Human beings were created in the 'image' of God and commanded to rule over other creatures (Genesis 1:26–28). In the same way as the viceroy was seen as the representative of the king in the ancient Near East, humans were deemed to be the representatives of God in the Genesis account. The rest of creation was entrusted to humans, not to exploit and destroy but to rule with mercy, love and real concern for the welfare of all (Psalm 72).[8] Humans were challenged to use wisely and sparingly the good things that God has created.

The Hebrew scriptures recognized that human beings, like all other animals, do not create their own energy. They are dependent on other creatures. The final paragraph of Wendell Berry's book *The Gift of Good Land* captures this point beautifully:

> To live we must daily break the body and shed the blood of creation. When we do this knowingly, lovingly, skilfully, and reverently it is a sacrament. When we do it ignorantly, greedily and destructively it is a desecration. In such a desecration we condemn ourselves to spiritual and moral loneliness and others to want.[9]

This notion of stewardship underlies many commendable practices which are found in the Mosaic Law, like the Sabbath rest for humans, animals and the land (Exodus 23:10–12), respect for breeding stock (Deuteronomy 22:6–7) and the prohibition on destroying fruit trees (Deuteronomy 20:19). Modern agriculture and labour practices would do well to take seriously once again the rhythms of the natural world and of human living.

The notion of stewardship is pervasive in Christian thinking and also in the modern planning paradigm. Nevertheless, it is important to recognize that there are a number of serious difficulties and dangers with this approach. Some recent studies, especially one by Clare Palmer, have raised serious questions about whether this concept is really suitable for addressing many of the complex issues raised by the contemporary ecological crisis.[10] She points out that in both the Hebrew and Christian Testament the notion of steward-ship appears in the context either of a steward looking after the master's property or, as in some of the New Testament parables, his money. They focus on the rights and responsibilities of a steward for his master's property (Daniel 1:11–20; Matthew 24:45–51). The master is perceived to be absent; so the steward is responsible for the running of the household in a fair and efficient way until the master returns.

The first difficulty with the stewardship analogy is that God is viewed as an absentee landlord who has put human beings in charge of the rest of creation. This implies that having created the world God has absented himself from its day-to-day activities and left this in the hands of humans. In addition, within the context of this analogy the earth is reified and becomes either inert property to be cared for or financial resources to be managed in a way that gives a good return on the investment. A reified earth, stripped of any divine presence, gives a very impoverished understanding of creation.

It is, needless to say, challenged from within the biblical tradition itself. The Bible affirms the presence and 'indwelling' of God in both humanity and in the rest of creation. In the words of the poet Gerard Manley Hopkins, 'The world is charged with the grandeur of God'. Psalm 19:1 declares that 'The heavens declare the glory of God; the vault of heaven proclaims his handiwork'. Yahweh also delights in creation itself (Genesis 1:10, 12, 17–18) even before the emergence of humans.

Nevertheless, the stewardship metaphor is unable to carry any overtones of the earth as the body of God that is so dear to some of the Hindu scriptures. The Isa Upanishad affirms that everything, from a blade of grass to the cosmos as a whole, is the home of God. God lives in every corner of existence, therefore the whole of creation is sacred.[11]

It is also true that Christian theology almost from its earliest days   𝄪
was so frightened of slipping into pantheism that it often, in
practice, forgot the immanence of God in creation. Nevertheless
the notion of the earth as the body of God is not completely lacking
in Christian theology. Thomas Aquinas in a moment of daring can
affirm that *sic est anima in corpore, sicut Deus in mundo* (God
dwells in the world in the same way as the soul dwells in the body).[12]

When this idea of the earth as the body of God is applied to the
notion of stewardship it becomes clear immediately how problematic the idea is from a variety of theological and ecological angles. It
envisages a God who exists outside creation. This Being contracts a
single, fairly recently evolved species, *homo sapiens*, to manage his/
her body on behalf of himself/herself or other humans, or future
generations of humans or the rest of creation. Which of those
different parties are the intended beneficiary of stewardship is not at
all clear. Like any other metaphor, this one has its limits. Daniel L.
Migliore in his book *Faith, Seeking Understanding* draws attention
to some of the limitations of metaphor of the earth as the body of
God. He suggests that it 'fails to depict appropriately either the
freedom of God in relation to the world or the real otherness and
freedom of the world'.[13]

Nevertheless it helps clarify the limitations inherent in the notion
of stewardship. Humans, in fact, have not managed the earth for the
good of the whole human community, not to mention the earth
community. Furthermore, much human interference with nature
has been extremely deleterious, mainly because it has been short-
sighted and oblivious of the impact on other creatures. Industrial
agriculture, for example, when practised on fragile crop land,
especially in the tropics, may initially produce large quantities of
food. But from the perspective of the forest, the topsoil and the
nearby river and estuary it is destructive. Consequently it will also
be a disaster for future generations when the soil is degraded and
unavailable to meet their needs.

  𝄪 Another danger associated with the stewardship analogy is that it
appears to give humans some proprietary rights over the rest of
creation. Once again this is challenged in the Bible. As the Psalmist
puts it: 'The earth is the Lord's, and the fullness thereof' (24:1). In
Leviticus it is clear that Yahweh too is the owner of the land: 'It [the
land] must not be sold in perpetuity, for the land belongs to me and
to me you are only strangers and guests' (25:23).

Stewardship also implies that nature is somehow incomplete
unless it is improved upon by human hands. Only when nature is

managed by humans, for example through cultivating a garden, does it begin to have any real significance. Human activity is usually seen as completing or perfecting raw nature. A landscape transformed by human hands and planted like a lawn, even in a country like Australia where water is scarce, is usually preferred to an untouched or natural habitat. This attitude has deep roots within the biblical tradition.

Frederick Turner in *Beyond Geography* insists that environmental factors must be taken into account in any attempt to understand the biblical perspective of the natural world.[14] In their efforts to survive in the Fertile Crescent, countless generations wrestled with nature to keep its destructive (from a human viewpoint) potential in check. They drained marshes, dug irrigation canals, terraced hillsides and built protective fortifications against marauding animals and hostile armies. All of this was considered necessary to support growing populations from the natural world. It was hard, back-breaking work and nature was often experienced as stubborn, capricious and un-co-operative. The pain, toil and effort is echoed in Genesis 3:17–19:

> Accursed shall be the soil because of you;
> Painfully you will get your food from it
> as long as you live.
> It will yield you brambles and thistles,
> as you eat the produce of the land.
> By the sweat of your face
> you will earn your food,
> until you return to the ground.

Contemporary English reflects this attitude towards nature, of always having to alter it before it becomes really significant. For example, we speak of a place where humans have left their imprint by building houses as a 'development' area. The first settlers in the United States and Australia justified taking land from the indigenous people because they were not engaged in agriculture and so were not seen to be using the land as God intended it to be used.

Given the poor track record which humans, especially those imbued with a European attitude, have towards the rest of creation, the heavy managerial overtones present in the notion of stewardship are not very helpful. Many fear that hidden in the stewardship analogy is a deep-seated hubris, that humans have the knowledge, ability and integrity to rearrange nature and improve on it.

Moreover, there is a feeling that the good steward can amass such a comprehensive knowledge of his/her subject, be it in the area of farm management or financial dealings, that his/her policies and projects would be truly constructive and beneficial.

The danger is that this viewpoint might spill over into one's stance towards the natural world; that one could fool oneself into thinking that a comprehensive knowledge of the natural world is also possible. But the living world of a rainforest, for example, is so complex, so interrelated, so delicately balanced that humans can never presume to have the thorough knowledge with which to manage the natural world in any comprehensive way. Any engagement with it, or effort to change it, should begin with this humble admission. The most recent and potentially disastrous area where this managerial ethos is evident is in the area of biotechnology and genetic engineering.

Palmer also criticizes the proposition that 'all created goods are directed to the good of humanity' as the most dangerous assumption contained in the idea of stewardship. 'If the natural world is like a huge bank account which we may use, however prudently, then environmental ethics which flows from this is entirely human-centred. Provided that something can be justified as benefiting humanity, or some segment of humanity, it is morally acceptable under a stewardship ethic.'[15] But even the Bible is clear on the fact that the *raison d'être* of creation is not found primarily in its ability to meet human needs. It has its own dignity, its own rights and reasons for being, quite apart from its role in sustaining humans.

Furthermore, Yahweh is not confined to acting in creation through the mediation of humans. The Bible asserts that Yahweh tends creation. S/he can and does reach into areas which are inaccessible to humans. Psalm 104:10–12 states: 'You set springs gushing in ravines, running down between the mountains; supplying water for wild animals, attracting the thirsty donkeys; there the birds of the air make their nests and sing among the branches.'

God is also present within creation. Yet, despite the traditional affirmations about the immanence of God in all reality, the Christian churches have been very wary of anything that smacks of pantheism. This over-reacting to God's abiding presence in the world has effectively removed God from creation, and firmly placed the Divine in transcendent reality. We need to redefine our idea of the Divine, not in terms of pantheism – which believes that God is confined to the phenomena of this world – but rather in terms of *panentheism*. This asserts that while God is present in all reality and all reality is in God, h/she also transcends the world.

This vision of God in all creation and all creation in God is precisely what is needed today in order to resanctify all of nature. While human beings will be seen to have a crucial place within this wider sacred community, the dignity and intrinsic value of other creatures will be acknowledged. Such a re-visioning will inevitably evoke a whole cluster of new relationships: those between human beings and God, interhuman relationships, and human relationships with the rest of creation. Within that larger framework the stewardship metaphor will be seen in its true context. It will become clear that it is not the only metaphor which Christians have to mediate our relationships with nature.

ECO-CENTRED ETHICS

The anthropocentric ethical norms of our Western humanist and religious traditions are not capable of addressing the challenges which the earth community now faces. Unfortunately in these traditions only humans have rights; other members of the earth community are mere instruments to be used by humans to meet their needs. The bottom line is that the earth is at the service of humans. It is crucial that this perspective be abandoned if further irreversible, ecological damage is to be avoided. Humans must broaden their horizons and begin to see themselves within the larger context of the earth, as an integral community of all living and non-living components. For Fr Tom Berry the domain of ethics 'concerns the manner whereby humans give expression at the rational level to the ethics of this larger community'. Berry contends that, if we are to have a proper ethical framework adequate for the present task, we must recognize that:

> The human community is subordinate to the ecological
> community. The ecological imperative is not derivative from
> human ethics. Human ethics is derivative from the ecological
> imperative. The basic ethical norm is the well-being of the
> comprehensive community, not the well-being of the human
> community. The earth is a single ethical system, as the
> universe itself is a single ethical system.[16]

Many Catholics who are concerned about the irreversible destruction of the environment which is rampant today will be saddened

that the environment does not even merit a single reference in the
encyclical *Veritatis Splendor* (*The Splendour of Truth*). Pope John
Paul II says he wrote the encyclical, issued on 6 August 1993, to
restate the essential elements of Catholic moral teaching in the light
of the confusion about moral values which he sees in the modern
world and even in the Church. It is a lengthy document which
should have provided ample opportunity to deal with one of the
most pressing contemporary moral issues, particularly since he
identified the environment crisis as a moral one in his 1990 World
Day of Peace message, *Peace with God the Creator, Peace with All
Creation* (nos 6 and 15). However, *Veritatis Splendor* completely
overlooks it.

The first line of the text 'The splendour of truth shines forth in all
the works of the Creator . . . ' provided an ideal opportunity to
reflect systematically on the morality of disfiguring the image of
God in creation. But this was not grasped. The encyclical deals with
the universal and unchanging nature of moral norms and restates
that particular moral acts like homicide, genocide, abortion,
contraception and euthanasia are intrinsically evil (nos 80 and 96).
The relationship between the human community and the wider
earth community, of which it is an integral part, is not mentioned.
The morality of sexual, political and economic behaviour is
discussed and clear norms enunciated. However there is no mention
of the morality of biocide or geocide; the poisoning of the air, water
and soil; or the irreversible destruction of crucial habitats like
rainforests.

It would seem that the drafters of the encyclical are so steeped in
the anthropocentric worldview that they are totally blind to the
moral implications of environmental destruction. Maybe they
believe that humans live in their own cocoon, cut off from and
unrelated to the rest of creation, rather than forming a single
community with all the living world. In the list of fundamental
questions: What is Man? What is the meaning and purpose of life?
(no. 30), the contemporary question about the human relationship
with the rest of creation ought to have been addressed. The
omission is all the more difficult to understand given some of the
Pope's statements on the environment and the importance which he
attaches to the human body as a determining element in judging the
morality of individual acts (nos 48, 49 and 67).

The discussion on natural law in nos 43 and 44 would have been
an appropriate place in which to discuss this theme. The Pope wrote
that 'in this way God calls man to participate in his own providence,

since he desires to guide the world – *not only the world of nature* but also the world of human persons – through man himself, through *man's reasonable and responsible care*' (emphasis mine). But the text slips back to focus exclusively on the human realm and the opportunity to address the wider issue is simply lost. This oversight in a document written so recently is tragic given the scale of worldwide environmental destruction and its continuing impact on all life, including the future of humanity.

Thankfully, other voices have attempted to address the ethics of environmental issues. One contemporary effort to widen ethical parameters happened in the wake of the *Exxon Valdez* disaster in 1989. A number of commercial companies, NGOs and churches came together and drew up a list of ethical principles called the Valdez Principles, which they pledge to use as a guide in their commercial activity. The first and most fundamental principle highlighted the need to protect the biosphere as the most basic goal of any human activity, including economic activity.

This concern for the well-being of the total biosphere is challenging the churches to engage in what the Australian theologian Elaine Wainwright calls the 'hermeneutics of reclamation'.[17] This involves identifying and developing those stories and themes in the biblical tradition which take a biocentric rather than a homocentric perspective on creation. A number of biblical scholars, among them Robert Murray, have been acutely aware of environmental questions in their research. Murray writes: 'I became convinced that the theology of creation, especially as it has developed among Christians, has improperly narrowed the scope and power of the Bible's teaching about our place and responsibilities in the world, at a time when it is needed as never before.'[18]

The Noah story (Genesis 6:11 – 9:17), for example, embodies a concern for the whole web of creation and therefore has a profound message for our modern world. Yahweh commanded Noah to conserve nature: 'From all living creatures, from all living things, you must take two of every kind aboard into the ark, to save their lives with yours; they must be male and female' (6:19). In the wake of the flood, Yahweh renewed the command of Genesis 1:28 to humans to 'be fruitful and multiply and fill the earth' (9:1). Even though humans were designated as the 'terror and the dread of all the wild beasts and all the birds of heaven, of everything that crawls on the ground and all the fish of the sea' (9:2), nevertheless after the flood Yahweh entered into a covenant, not just with Noah and his family, but with future generations and *all* creation:

> God spoke to Noah and his sons. 'I am now establishing my
> covenant with you and with your descendants to come, and
> with every living creature that was with you; birds, cattle and
> every wild animal with you, everything that came out of the
> ark. . . . And this', God said, 'is the sign of the covenant
> which I now make between myself and you and every living
> creature with you for all ages to come: I now set my bow in
> the clouds and it will be a sign of the covenant between me
> and the earth.' (9:8–13)

For Robert Murray the Noah text involves a cosmic covenant
(Genesis 9:8–17) which 'binds humans and animals together as the
Creator's partners'. For him it cannot be adequately understood
within either the model of the Mosaic covenant in Exodus or the
covenant between Yahweh and the house of David in 2 Samuel 7. In
the Noah covenant Yahweh, human beings and the rest of creation
are all included.[19]

This linking of the covenant with creation has been taken up by
the Justice, Peace and the Integrity of Creation (JPIC) programme
of the World Council of Churches (WCC). At their 1990 Convocation in Seoul four areas were selected for acts of covenanting:

- A just economic order and liberation from the bondage of debt.
- The security of all nations and peoples.
- The building of a culture that can live in harmony with creation's
  integrity.
- The eradication of racism and discrimination, on the national and
  international level, among all peoples.

Churches which are members of the World Council of Churches and
even those which are not, like the Roman Catholic Church, are
encouraged to promote these covenants in the JPIC programme.

The Wisdom literature is also full of references to God's
knowledge of and care for all creatures. Solomon's knowledge of
the flora and fauna is seen as a sign of his wisdom (1 Kings 4:33–34).
The book of Job also has a theocentric and biocentric focus.
Humans are not the only creatures on the divine agenda. Nowhere
is this more forcibly stated than in the speeches of Yahweh in
chapters 38 to 41. We get a flavour of this in chapter 38, where
Yahweh challenges and chides Job's arrogance and conceit:

> Where were you when I laid the foundations of the earth?

> Tell me, if you have understanding.
> Who determined its measurements? – surely you know!
> Or who stretched the line upon it?
> On what were its bases sunk,
> or who laid its cornerstone,
> when the morning stars sang together,
> and all the sons of God shouted for joy?
> Or who shut in the sea with doors
> when it burst forth from the womb;
> when I made clouds its garment
> and thick darkness its swaddling band,
> and prescribed bounds for it
> and set bars and doors,
> and said, 'Thus far shall you come,
> and no farther;
> and here shall your proud waves be stayed'?
> (38:4–11)

Chapter 38 continues to deal not with the world of human history, but with the world of nature in its beginnings and vital processes. Yahweh demands to know whether the proud Job understands or can account for all the phenomena of nature. He goes on to assert that his creation is meant to serve other creatures also. Other creatures have their legitimate needs and Yahweh, as the Creator and sustainer of all, has provided them with their unique habitats:

> Who has cleft a channel for the torrents of rain,
> and a way for the thunderbolt,
> to bring rain on a land where no man is,
> on the desert in which there is no man;
> to satisfy the waste and desolate land
> and to make the ground put forth grass?
> (38:25–27)

> Who has let the wild ass go free?
> Who has loosed the bonds of the swift ass,
> to whom I have given the steppe for his home,
> and the salt flats for his dwelling place?
> (39:5–6)

Gustavo Gutiérrez's comment on the above texts in his book *On Job* really sums up my point:

God's speeches are a forceful rejection of a purely anthropocentric view of creation. Not everything that exists was made directly useful to human beings; therefore they may not judge everything from their point of view. The world of nature expresses the freedom and delight of God in creation.[20]

The book of Job charts his progression from being fixated on his own pain to empathizing with fellow sufferers to appreciating God as the author of all creation. Job's journey, painful as it was for him, helped to transform him from a self-centred person into one who is sensitive to others, especially the weak and oppressed. He also developed a much deeper appreciation of who God really is and how s/he relates in an ongoing way to all creation. This transformation enriches Job's life immensely.

Christians today must make this same journey. It will involve breaking out of the narrow anthropocentric perspective on which much of our economic, educational, social, political, technological and even religious activities are based.

Christians and all religious people can be helped immeasurably by the insights of Fr Thomas Berry. In his books *The Dream of the Earth* and *The Universe Story* (which he has written with Brian Swimme) Berry uses the insights of physicists, biologists and other scientists, especially Teilhard de Chardin, to tell the story of our emergent universe.[21] He charts the extraordinary unbroken sequence of transformations which have led from the initial cosmic flaring forth to the birth of a creative genius like Beethoven.

During the past two centuries scientists have articulated the story as one involving the transformation of matter and life. Berry insists that there is also a deep, inner dimension to all reality which intensifies as creation becomes more diversified. But diversity and an inner dimension are not the final words about creation. All creation is bonded together into a single community. For Berry this new story of the emergence of our earth must become the norm of reality and the central value for every other activity. It invites humans to enter more deeply into the dynamics of creation and ensures that their activities are in tune with the rhythms of creation instead of exploiting and destroying it. All of the religious traditions, including the biblical one, will find their contemporary meaning within the context of this larger story.[22]

This fresh interpretation of the biblical tradition will help us to encode new ethical principles which capture this vision of the earth existing and surviving only in its integral functioning. These principles will enable us to recognize the absolute evil of biocide and geocide and the immorality of pursuing policies which irreversibly damage the life-support system of the planet. While it is crucial to be concerned about the human right to habitats within a particular region, the rights of other creatures to their habitats must also be respected. This is in contrast to the Holy See's submission to the Rio Summit which argued that 'the ultimate determining factor is the human person'. Tom Berry insists that;

> the earth is primary and that humans are derivative. The present distortion is that the humans are primary and the earth and its integral functioning can only be secondary. Thus the pathology manifest in our various human institutions, professions, programmes and activities. The only acceptable way for humans to function effectively is by giving first consideration to the earth community and then dealing with humans as integral members of that community.[23]

This does not mean abandoning the traditional Christian insistence on the dignity and value of the human person and opting for what some call a 'biospheric democracy'. But it does mean respecting the intrinsic value of other creatures and acting accordingly.

THE EXAMPLE OF THE COSMIC CHRIST

It would be a distortion to pretend that care for creation is a central theme of the Gospel of Jesus. Nevertheless a Christian theology of creation can learn much from the attitude of respect which Jesus displayed towards the natural world. He enjoyed an intimacy with nature which is evident from his parables – the sower and the seed (Matthew 13:3–9, 18–23), the vine and the branches (John 15:1–17; Mark 12:1–12). He illustrated his stories by referring to the lilies of the field (Luke 12:27), the birds of the air (Matthew 6:26), and foxes and their lairs (Luke 9:58).

In this age of unbridled consumerism it is important to remember that Jesus lived lightly on the earth. He warned his disciples against hoarding possessions and allowing their hearts to be enticed by the lure of wealth (Matthew 6:19–21). This acquisitiveness, which Jesus called 'mammon', has been glorified by modern, commercial culture and promoted aggressively by the media. The result is a throw-away, earth-destroying and grossly unjust society, far removed from the teachings of Jesus or any other of the great religious teachers.

Christians down through the centuries have heard the call of Jesus to follow him. The values that Jesus promoted, the attitude which he espoused, and his behaviour towards others are crucial for Christians. However the answer to every modern question is not necessarily to be found in the New Testament. Problems of toxic waste, acid rain, chemical agriculture, forest destruction or rapid population growth did not exist during the lifetime of Jesus, or at least were not seen as crucial for the survival of the earth and the human community. There are no ready-made answers to these challenges within the scriptures. Having said that, it would be a disservice to the living word of God to allow ourselves to be paralysed or hemmed in by the literal interpretation of individual gospel texts, and not try to answer these questions out of the context of a living faith. The challenge for the Christian is to be 'rooted and grounded in him' (Colossians 2:7) 'who came to bring life and give it to the full' (John 10:10), and thus to respond in a creative way to the challenges facing us today.

In the light of contemporary challenges it is crucial to stress that the Christian tradition does not despise material goods. It affirms the goodness of God's creation, gives thanks for its fruitfulness and rejoices in its beauty. It recognizes that God is the source of life for all creation, not just for human beings. Furthermore it affirms that God's glory is manifested in all things, and that it is in and through the communion and combined voices of all creatures that God's name is properly praised. In order to be in harmony with all of creation humans need to develop the inner freedom which will liberate them from greed and the insatiable desire to accumulate. This demands a restraint in the use of material goods similar to that found in the life of Jesus. In a very real way the present ecological crisis gives new meaning and urgency to the Gospel's invitation to simplicity of life.

Considering how humans are inflicting enormous damage on the biosphere and creating a sick planet, Christian theology of redemption needs to expand its focus to include all creation. While there are glimpses of this in the New Testament (Romans 8:18–25), the weight of redemption theology in both the Eastern and the Western tradition is centred on human beings. This stance is reflected in the treatment of redemption in the new *Catechism of the Catholic Church* (nos 599–618). The non-human world does not appear. It states that 'Christ's death is both the Paschal sacrifice that accomplishes the definitive redemption for men, through "the Lamb of God who takes away the sin of the world" ' (no. 613).

In some churches, especially those associated with early Celtic Christianity, nature was involved in the drama of redemption. In a commentary on the Anglo-Saxon poem 'The Dream of the Cross' Robert Murray contends that it goes beyond the theme of cosmic and creaturely compassion for the suffering servant but 'dares to entrust the expression of Christ's suffering to the voice of a dumb creature. The effect is that the Cross's pain stands for the pain of all creatures, with which St Paul saw all creation groaning (Romans 8:19–22).' The tree is united with Christ in his agony:

> They mocked us together. I was soaked in
> the blood streaming from the man's side
> after he set his spirit free.
> I underwent many horrors on that hill.
> I was the God of hosts stretched on the rack.
> Clouds of darkness gathered over the corpse
> of the Ruler; the shadows, black shapes
> under the clouds, swept across
> his shining splendour. All creation wept,
> at the King's death, Christ was on the cross.[24]

Finally, it is important to remember that the centrality of Jesus is not confined to reflecting on his behaviour during his short life on earth. We are resurrection people. Jesus is, as Paul tells us in Colossians 3:11 and many similar texts, the centre of human and cosmic history:

> For he has made known to us in all wisdom and insight the mystery of his will according to the purpose which he set forth in Christ as a plan for the fullness of time, to unite all things in him, things in heaven and things on earth. (Ephesians 1:9–10)

Christ was active before time began in bringing forth creation. Through him the universe, the earth and all life was created (John 1:3–5). All the rich unfolding of the story of the universe – from the initial glow of the flaring forth, through the shaping of the elements in the cauldron of the stars and the positioning of the earth in a way that allowed it to become the green planet of the universe, right up to the emergence of humans and their varied cultures and histories – is centred on Jesus (Colossians 1:16–17).

Christians often make the mistake of thinking that the resurrection somehow catapults Jesus out of the order of creation and places him in some atemporal zone. The New Testament is adamant that the risen Christ is even more deeply centred in all creation. The preface for the Mass of Easter Day rejoices in the fact that the resurrection 'renews all creation'. Every living creature on earth has a profound relationship with the resurrected Lord. His loving touch heals our brokenness and fulfils all creation. So, to wantonly destroy any aspect of creation or to banish species for ever from their place in the community of life is to deface the image of Christ which is radiated throughout our world.

CHRISTIAN HOPE

Church leaders and ministers are most likely to soft-pedal the harsh realities of environmental devastation when their constant focus on the environmental challenge may be construed as a message of despair. The Swiss theologian Lukas Vischer put his finger on this danger in *Concilium*: 'For are they [the churches] not expected to be a treasury of hope in this time of uncertainty and anxiety? The churches are easily misled by this pressure and as a result blur the challenge by religious statements about hope. But the freedom which the Gospel brings must be shown precisely in the way in which Christians can face reality.'[25]

Faced with this contemporary challenge Christians are, undoubtedly, called to be bearers of hope in today's world. The gospels proclaim this hope as one of the basic gifts of the Spirit of God. The gift of hope, for both individuals and Christian communities, is sorely needed today. This hope involves both recognizing the present crisis for what it is and acknowledging that the lubricated pathways of much of modernity are leading to death. This is how the prophet Jeremiah responded to the denial and self-deception which he saw all around him in the Israel of his day. True hope empowers people to witness to the truth of the present situation, especially when the leadership of society speak hollow words of peace when death and disintegration are already in the air.

The honesty and clarity which comes from exposing the present illusion of prosperity can also provide the spiritual energy which is needed to address the ecological crisis in realistic ways. Authentic hope admonishes Christians that they must be wary of many of the reductionist conceptions of hope which are alive in today's world. It goes way beyond the cynical posture of believing that nothing new can ever happen, that one should grit one's teeth and accept 'what will be, will be'.

Genuine hope does not encourage the religious person to seek solace and reassurance in the present confusion by relying on a fundamentalist interpretation of scriptural texts. This, unfortunately, is rife in almost every organized religion today. It is essential that any presentation of Christian hope or eschatology should not diminish a Christian's commitment to this world. Some Christians, for example, misread 2 Peter 3 and find therein predictions about the future annihilation of the earth. It is important for Christians to remember that the vision of a new heaven and new earth described in Revelation 21 is meant to intensify the commitment of Christians to promoting the Kingdom of God on earth.

Neither is hope to be found in attempting to escape the present historical challenge by opting for a privatized, spiritual, other-worldly religion that jettisons social concerns and concentrates attention on future happiness in heaven. Christians who emphasize their personal relationship with Christ and exclude everything else cut themselves off from the cry of the poor and the groanings of creation. In doing this they ignore two essential elements of authentic hope. The first is a sense of solidarity in suffering which stems from experiencing the contemporary agony of the poor and the pathos of the ecological crisis. The second is that any sincere conversion and consequent commitment to living a simple lifestyle will inevitably involve giving up luxuries and accepting discomfort.

Once hope is cast within a social and ecological context it will free the individual and collective Christian imagination from the tyranny of the present order. This order, as I have repeatedly stressed, excludes so many people from the table of life and forces them to live in penury, squalor and hopelessness. The willingness to dream about new vistas will give renewed energy to those who see the future as an open gift of a gracious God. It will give them the courage to set about the task of discovering new ways in which to live in fellowship with all humankind and with all creation. It will allow Christians, perhaps especially young people, to devote their talents, energy and commitment to doing new things. In this way they can face and surmount the contemporary mood of despair and thus discover a direction for their lives, rather than surrendering to the ebb and flow of an aimless tide.

Ultimately hope in new possibilities is grounded in a belief in the God of new life who, against all the odds, freed Israel from slavery, raised Jesus from the dead and is still active in our world. This hope is the inspiration of Isaiah, who counsels:

> No need to recall the past,
> no need to think about what was done before.
> See, I am doing a new deed,
> even now it comes to light; can you not see it?
> (43:18–19)

Finally, one important Christian notion captures the urgency of the task which faces us. There are a number of words for 'time' in Greek, among them *chronos* and *kairos*. *Chronos* connotes time as a succession of moments counted in some orderly way. The word 'chronology' is derived from this Greek word. The New Testament seldom uses this word and prefers to use *kairos*. In the term *kairos* the focus is on the meaning of this particular, special moment. It is normally understood as a moment of crisis wherein lies great potential for good or evil. The antipathy between the forces of good and evil is seen to be coming to a climax and people are challenged to make a choice. The ultimate resolution of the conflict is assured since Yahweh is in charge of the world, but the contemporary challenges presented demand the active involvement of believers. For many individuals and groups this will mean a conversion experience. The ecological crisis is such a *kairos* moment.

In an address to the American Institute of Biological Sciences in August 1988 the biologist Thomas Lovejoy said that 'I am utterly convinced that most of the great environmental struggles will either be won or lost in the 1990s. By the next century it will be too late.'[26] This states the challenge very clearly and underlines the *kairos* moment we are living in. Responding to it demands concrete choices for individuals and institutions to help bring about this new age. The Church, which Vatican II sees 'as a sign raised up among the nations', should be with the vanguard accompanying those who are trying to usher in this new, ecological age.

NOTES

1 Quoted in David Noble, *A World Without Women: The Christian Clerical Culture of Western Science* (Oxford: Oxford University Press, 1992), p. 221.
2 Keith Thomas, *Man and the Natural World* (New York: Pantheon Books, 1983), p. 35.
3 Clive Ponting, *A Green History of the World* (London: Sinclair-Stevenson, 1991), p. 142.
4 Lynn White, 'Historical roots of our ecological crisis', *Science* (1967).

5   Ted F. Peters, *The Cry of the Environment* (Santa Fe: Bear, 1984), pp. 415–16.

6   Robert Goodland and Herman Daly, 'Ten reasons why Northern income growth is not the solution to Southern poverty' (private circulation, 1992: Environment Department, World Bank, Washington DC 20433), p. 4.

7   'Come Holy Spirit, renew the whole creation', address to the World Council of Churches, Seventh Assembly, Canberra, Australia (7–20 February 1991).

8   Robert Murray SJ, 'The relationship of creatures with the cosmic covenant', *The Month* (November 1990), p. 425. See also, by the same author, *The Cosmic Covenant*, a Heythrop Monograph (London: Sheed and Ward, 1992).

9   Wendell Berry, *The Gift of Good Land* (San Francisco: North Point Press, 1981), p. 281.

10 Clare Palmer, 'Stewardship: a case study in environmental ethics' in Ian Hall, Margaret Goodall, Clare Palmer and John Reader (eds), *The Earth Beneath: A Critical Guide to Green Theology* (London: SPCK, 1992).

11 Ranchor Prime, *Hinduism and Ecology* (London: Cassell, 1992), p. 72.

12 Thomas Aquinas, *Summa Theologica*, I-II, c. 17 a. 8 ad 2, quoted in 'Towards an ecological consciousness: Religious, ethical and spiritual perspectives', *Vidya-jyoti Journal of Theological Reflection*, vol. LV, no. 9 (September 1991), pp. 489–501.

13 Daniel L. Migliore, *Faith, Seeking Understanding* (Grand Rapids, MI: Eerdmans, 1991), p. 93.

14 Frederick Turner, *Beyond Geography: The Western Spirit Against the Wilderness* (New York: Viking, 1980).

15 Clare Palmer, op. cit., p. 81.

16 Thomas Berry, 'Ethics and ecology', unpublished paper (1994).

17 Elaine Wainwright, 'A metaphorical walk through scripture in an ecological age', *Pacifica*.

18 Robert Murray, *The Cosmic Covenant*, op. cit., p. xvii.

19 Ibid., p. 427.

20 Gustavo Gutiérrez, *On Job: God Talk and the Suffering of the Innocent* (Quezon City, Philippines: Claretian Publications, 1986), p. 74.

21 Thomas Berry and Brian Swimme, *The Universe Story* (San Francisco: HarperCollins, 1992).

22 Thomas Berry, 'The New Story' in *The Dream of the Earth* (San Francisco: Sierra Club Books, 1988), pp. 123–38.

23 Thomas Berry, 'The ecozoic era', E. F. Schumacher Society lecture (October 1991), unpublished.

24 Robert Murray, 'Tradition and originality in "The Dream of the Cross" ', *The Month* (May 1994), pp. 177–84.

25 Lukas Vischer, 'What about the garden? The ecological dimension of the European home', *Concilium*, no. 2 (1992).

26 Quoted in Lester Brown et al. (eds), *The State of the World 1989* (Washington DC: Worldwatch Institute, 1989), p. 192.

CHAPTER **8**

A pastoral ministry of sustainability

Ecological concerns must now move from the distant, almost non-existent periphery to centre stage in the pastoral ministry of the churches. It is difficult to spell out what this might involve as the demands of each bioregion will be different. A few brief pointers might help chart the way for the Church as it strives to accompany other groups and communities who are attempting to change their pattern of living and live more lightly on the earth.

RENEWING LITURGY AND DEVOTIONS

The Church should recognize the transformative power that liturgy and worship have in addressing the ecological and justice crisis. Good ritual can help communities evolve a new mode of human interaction with other human beings and the natural world. Since the emergence of human beings on earth, women and men have always sought to express the deepest mysteries of their own life and the rhythms of the earth and cosmos through myths, rituals and ceremonies. Robert Murray believes that Israel shared with her near neighbours a 'belief in a divinely willed order harmoniously linking heaven and earth'.[1] Ceremonies to celebrate this cosmic covenant and to dispel disruptive, hostile forces were important in Israel's religious life.[2]

Such ceremonies are even more vital today. Nevertheless it is important to recognize that sacramental religion is not easy. Modern human beings, and especially modern Christians, are caught in the double bind of being alienated from the natural world and of having become accustomed to worshipping in a way that spiritualizes the sacraments. In comparison to tribal people like the T'boli, Western people often feel alienated from the natural world. The T'boli live in communion with the universe: their rising and sleeping are dictated by the dawn and sunset; their agricultural practices follow the seasons. They are aware of the stars and the phases of the moon, and are moved in a striking way by a natural phenomenon like an eclipse or an earthquake.

Most people in the industrialized world, on the other hand, have lost this contact with nature. As Fr Thomas Berry puts it: 'We hardly live in a universe at all. We live in a city or nation, in an economic system, in a cultural tradition. . . . We live in a world of objects not subjects. We isolate ourselves from contact with the natural world except in so far as we enjoy it or have command over it. The natural world is not associated with the very meaning of life.'[3]

The sacraments which draw on the elements of the natural world – water, food, oil, fire, light, darkness and wind – and facilitate our encounter with the Divine should be able to draw us out of our false cocoon and reconnect us with God and creation. Unfortunately, as Bernard J. Cooke has pointed out in his painstaking work on the sacraments *The Distancing of God*, the sacramental signs and the theology which imbues them with meaning have often been used to distance rather than mediate the divine presence.[4] In the light of a growing awareness of ecological issues there is a need to reverse this process and to revise the rituals, symbols, narratives and prayers associated with the various sacraments so that modern Christians may experience, in a more forceful way, our interconnection with all creation and our call to genuine stewardship. One could also realistically hope that this search for appropriate liturgies would spark a new period of creativity among Christians in music, dance, poetry, sculpture and the composition of sacred texts.

Local churches and the universal Church might imitate the Orthodox Church and institute a Feast of Creation. At present Catholic liturgies celebrate historical events associated with the mystery of Christ, Our Lady and the witness of the saints within the renewing cycles of nature. As yet we have no liturgy to celebrate the original moment of the emergence of the universe from the fireball or other pivotal 'cosmological moments of grace' as Fr Thomas Berry calls them. We do not mark the creation of the heavy elements in the cauldron of the supernova explosions, the shaping of our solar system, the emergence of life on earth, the blossoming of the flowers, the appearance of mammals or even *homo sapiens*. All these are part of our story but we do not commemorate them in ritual.

This is one of the most striking differences between modern Western culture and more traditional societies. Most traditional religions celebrate the moment of origin as the sacred moment for the tribe. These rituals guide the society in its relations with the gods, other humans and the earth. It would seem appropriate that we Catholics, who in the first line of our creed affirm that 'We believe in God, the Father Almighty, Creator of heaven and earth', should remind ourselves constantly of the gift of creation and of its present plight, both locally and globally.

In a world where water is being polluted and wasted the sacrament of baptism highlights the connection between living water and the power of the Spirit who incorporates those who are baptized into the Body of Christ. The parameters of this community into which the child is to be baptized must also be expanded to include the wider community of humanity and all creation.

Fr Vincent Busch, a missionary on the island of Mindanao in the Philippines, has attempted to do this. He has augumented the conventional baptismal ritual by introducing prayers and symbols from the natural world. After the normal ritual is completed in the church the child, parents, baptismal sponsors and local community are invited to move outside the church building into the cathedral of creation. In order to highlight the plight of what remains of the tropical rainforest the community is invited to form a circle around a number of tree saplings. The party is then divided into four units, each with the task of representing elements of the natural world – the soil, the sea, the forest and the sky. A representative of the parish asks these communities to accept the newborn baby with words like the following:

Rejoice you creatures of the soil for we have a new companion in our community. Celebrate their presence among us and do not fear them because they have promised to nurture God's living world. Rejoice you earthworms and soil bacteria because these children will co-operate with you in restoring the land's fertility.

The texts recognize that the earth community supports and nourishes all life including the newborn child. Someone who is known for his or her care for the earth responds on behalf of the earth community:

> We joyfully accept this child and as a sign of our commitment to protect, nurture and celebrate the community we live in, we bestow on these trees soil made fertile by our care.

This person then spreads some soil from a compost bucket on to the saplings. The ceremony continues with other members of the community offering gifts to the young trees from the community of the sea, the sky and the forest. Finally the young trees are given to the parents of the child. They are admonished in the following words:

> Dear friends, the Christian community gives you these trees to celebrate your belonging to us. Like these trees you will also need water, food, protection and sunlight in order to grow and mature. May the God of creation who sustains and renews all things through the miracle of the natural world guide you to live in harmony with the earth that gives you life. Amen.

This ceremony, which is modelled on a child initiation ceremony of the Omaha Indians in the United States, challenges this generation of Filipinos to protect what remains of the rainforest, the mangrove forests and the coral reefs. In my book *To Care for the Earth* I also describe an earth liturgy and a water liturgy which I used among the T'boli people in Mindanao.[5]

The Eucharist is also pregnant with all kinds of creative possibilities for deepening our awareness of the holy communion which unites God, human beings and all creation. In the Eucharist the elements of bread and wine, taken from the earth, are offered in the memory of the passion, death and resurrection of Christ and thereby transformed into his body and blood. The experience of the Eucharist challenges Christians to work for a just society, where food is shared and everyone has enough. It also summons Christians to work for a sustainable society, where the bonds of interdependence are more clearly understood, experienced and protected.

In a *Cross Currents* article 'Eucharistic ecology and ecological spirituality' Beatrice Bruteau writes about the earth as a eucharistic planet: 'a good gift planet which is structured as mutual feeding, as intimate self-sharing. It is a great Process, a circulation of living energies, in which the Real Presence of the Absolute is descerned.'[6] She goes on to write that the:

> various aspects of the universe can give themselves freely to one another because they have no need to preserve themselves, to save themselves for themselves. This is eucharistic ecology, and it is the ideal of all spiritual traditions. The Life of the Whole continues because all parties give themselves to it by giving themselves to each other. The dynamic interconnections in turn sustain all participants.[7]

The Eucharist is the holy communion in which all the members give themselves to one another in order to promote abundant life for all. Those who celebrate the Eucharist animated by such a vision would be expected to relate in a much more sensitive way to other creatures and to the earth as a whole.

The sacrament of reconciliation could provide a community with an opportunity to focus on the moral implications of injustice and environmental destruction. Through the experience of appropriate prayers and symbols incorporated into a rite of penance, individuals and the community as a whole could seek God's forgiveness for the damage which they were doing to the local and global environment. The collective examination of conscience might spotlight how individuals and the society as a whole use energy; whether they try to live simply; whether they waste resources; and finally, whether they purchase and use dangerous chemicals.

Fr Vincent Busch has also developed an ecological catechesis around traditional devotions like the Stations of the Cross and the Rosary. He produced a set of slides with an accompanying tape entitled *Stations of the Cross of the Death of the Forest*. This stark, challenging presentation presents the pain of the earth in the context of the suffering, death and resurrection of Christ. It anticipated the insight contained in *Peace with God the Creator, Peace with All Creation*. In that document the Pope states that 'The profound sense that the earth is "suffering" is also shared by those who do not profess our faith in God' (no. 5).

More recently Fr Busch has turned his attention to the fifteen decades of the Rosary. Below are three of the decades, which give a flavour of how he weaves in concerns for justice and the environment. His locus of concern is the ecosystems of north-west Mindanao in the Philippines; however any religious leader can use the same approach and incorporate the justice, peace and ecology challenges of their particular area.

THE ANNUNCIATION

The angel Gabriel was sent from God to a town of Galilee called Nazareth. He was sent to a young virgin who was engaged to a man named Joseph, of the family of David; and the virgin's name was Mary.

The angel came to her and said, 'Rejoice, full of grace, the Lord is with you. You shall conceive and bear a son and you shall call him Jesus. He will be great and shall rightly be called the Son of the Most High.'

Then Mary said, 'I am the servant of the Lord, let it be done to me as you have said.' (Luke 1:26–28, 31–32, 38)

THE ANNUNCIATION OF THE UNIVERSE

Billions of years ago the universe began with a tremendous explosion. Every being that has existed and will exist, every event that has happened and will happen belongs to the unfolding story of that exploding fireball. In the Bible story Mary belongs to the tribe of Israel and is engaged to Joseph, of the family of David. In the story of the universe, our shining sun, its planets and their moons are members of a celestial family called the solar system and that family belongs to a swirling tribe of stars called the Milky Way. Our galactic tribe and its solar family ride the expanding universe with countless star-building galaxies.

God has looked kindly on creation. From the moment of its explosive birth, the universe was empowered to bring all things into being. In communion with every pebble and planet we can retrace the sequence of events that moulded the earth and greened the land, that shaped the galaxies and light the stars back to that blazing instant when creation began, there to behold the Annunciation, 'Rejoice, O graced universe, God is with you'. We Christians can joyfully serve the Lord of the earth and sky by walking humbly with our God on the journey of creation.

THE CROWNING WITH THORNS

The Roman soldiers took Jesus into the palace of the governor and the whole troop gathered around him. They stripped off his clothes and dressed him in a purple military cloak. Then twisting a crown of thorns they forced it onto his head, and placed a reed in his right hand. They knelt before Jesus and mocked him, saying, 'Long life to the King of the Jews!' They spat on him, took the reed from his hand and struck him on the head with it. When they had finished mocking him, they pulled the purple cloak off and dressed him in his own clothes and led him out to be crucified. (Matthew 27:27–31)

MINDANAO IS CROWNED WITH ITS OWN THORNS

The soldiers stripped Jesus, dressed him in a purple cloak, forced thorns onto his head, and mockingly spat on him. Dressed in fancy words like 'progress' and 'development' money-serving policies and politics have stripped Mindanao's forests, seas and farms, and have poisoned its air, water, soil and people. But what kind of 'progress' and 'development' allows logging activities that destroy the forests, erode the soil, flood the lowlands, silt the seas, and impoverish the people? What kind of 'progress' and 'development' permits mining operations to scar the earth and to spew toxic waste into the seas and rivers? What kind of 'progress' and 'development' encourages farmers and agribusinesses to grow export crops rather than food for people? What kind of 'progress' and 'development' furthers the destruction of the bountiful mangrove swamps that provide basic food and fuel for coastal barrios, in favour of constructing shrimp ponds to gratify the appetites of the well-fed? What kind of 'progress' and 'development' promises employment in polluting industries that poison the future?

After abusing and mocking Jesus the soldiers led him out to be crucified. Are we asking our soldiers to protect 'progress' and 'development' that is crucifying Mindanao and its people?

THE ASSUMPTION OF JESUS CHRIST

When the Son of Man comes in his glory, with all his angels, he will sit on the throne of glory. All the nations will be brought before him. The King will say to those on his right, 'Come, blessed of my Father! Take possession of the Kingdom prepared for you from the beginning of the world. For I was hungry and you fed me. . . . I was sick and you visited me. I was in prison and you went to see me.' (Matthew 25:31–32, 34–36)

THE EARTH IS THE MIRACLE OF GOD'S COMPASSION

With these words Jesus welcomed his compassionate mother who fed, sheltered, clothed and nursed him, and stood by him during his passion and death. With these same words, the Lord will welcome all compassionate people into the reign of God.

We can be compassionate because we live on a generous and forgiving planet. We can feed the hungry because the earth's food cycle faithfully renews the bounty of the land and the seas. We can give drink to the thirsty because the earth's water cycle graciously replenishes its lakes, rivers, streams and springs. We can shelter the homeless because the hospitable earth mends its damaged habitats. We can comfort the sick because the healing earth continually refreshes and purifies its air, water and soil. We can lift up imprisoned hearts and minds because the life cycle of creation renews the wonders of the earth and sky.

Today, economic greed is killing our generous earth. Our topsoil is eroded, and our rivers and seas are sick with silt and pollution. In northwest Mindanao, in the Philippines, some Christian communities have taken compassion on the wounded earth and are nursing it back to life. Parents, catechists and children care for the earth the way Mary cared for Jesus. Using earth-sensitive prayers, songs, readings and symbols they also create liturgies that celebrate the dependency on the living world. Christ will welcome these caring communities into the Kingdom because they nurtured, protected and praised the miracle of God's compassion.

PROMOTING AND EDUCATING A NEW, SUSTAINABLE CULTURE

Moving beyond the liturgy, environmental issues must become part of the wider pastoral ministry of the Church. It is sad and ironic that the present ecological crisis is a result of considerable human success. Everyone will admit that greed, covetousness and other commonly recognized human vices have undoubtedly contributed to our present impasse. Nevertheless, the major cause of ecological devastation in our world today has been the unrelenting pursuit of what many people consider a good and desirable thing – the modern, growth-oriented, industrial model of development. What many people accept as the good life – something to be yearned for and aspired to – is in fact destroying the world. The most basic critique of this modern 'development' ideology is that it is not available to everyone, but it is also totally unsustainable.

The most crucial challenge for the Church today is to help people see beyond the glitter of this 'development' paradigm. Rather than creating a world full of plenty for everyone it has encouraged a culture of exploitation and death. The Church must work assiduously with those who are attempting to oppose this, and shape a new, compassionate and sustainable culture which is designed to support and enhance *all* life. So far the Catholic pro-life stance has been understood almost exclusively in the domain of sexual ethics. However it needs to embrace the good of the whole earth community. Only something as radical as that can truly claim to be pro-life.

Traditional Christian asceticism needs to be restated and encouraged. In the early monastic period simplicity of life was associated with temperance and charity. (Unfortunately, at times the traditional exhortations to simplicity were often associated with what appeared to be a world-negating ideology.) This call to simple living and avoidance of acquisitive greed is present in the scriptures. Jesus encourages people to 'seek first the Kingdom of God' (Matthew 6:33) and to 'store treasure in heaven' (Matthew 6:20). He warns against attempting to 'serve two masters . . . God and mammon' (Matthew 6:24).

The Church's call today to live both simply and in harmony with nature arises from our understanding of the seriousness of the ecological crisis and our new sense of Christian responsibility towards all creation. This spirituality must promote a spirit of non-acquisitiveness, of sharing, and of harmonious relationships at the interhuman level and between humans and the rest of creation. In *Peace with God the Creator, Peace with All Creation* Pope John Paul II calls for simplicity, moderation and discipline. In no. 13 he states that:

> Modern society will find no solution to the ecological problem unless it *takes a look at its lifestyle*. In many parts of the world society is given to instant gratification and consumerism while remaining indifferent to the damage which these cause. . . . Simplicity, moderation, and discipline must become a part of

everyday life, lest all suffer the negative consequence of the careless habits of a few.

Barbara Wood, writing in the *CAFOD Newsletter*, cites five guidelines for simple living.[8] This way of life:

- Leaves time and space for prayer.
- Is without waste.
- Reduces violence in our lives in the way we eat and travel.
- Encourages us to do more for ourselves.
- Reminds us that other generations will live on this earth also.

One practical example of a change to a simpler life was recently highlighted. Writing in the *Guardian* (1 April 1994) Professor Tim Chappell, an Oxford University philosopher, argues that 'Our society as a whole is addicted to the motor car in a way analogous to, but even more damaging than, the way in which individuals can be addicted to cigarettes'. He insists that this addiction is 'gravely damaging our society's health in multiple ways'. He continues: 'The tin god which sits in the garage governs, insidiously, far more of our attitudes and our priorities than we realize.' Since the only effective way to deal with an addiction – be it gambling, tobacco, or alcohol – is to give up that behaviour, Professor Chappell recommends that a 'very large portion of us [car-owners] should give up the private motor car completely, right now'. He does not see giving up a car as a moral imperative for everyone but as 'a morally superogatory choice, a free choice to respond to the stupidity, destruction, pollution and wastefulness of cars'. In an effort to start a Car-Free Movement he himself takes a pledge in the article to become car-free.

Making choices like this – be it giving up the use of a private car, or cutting down or avoiding meat altogether because of either cruel or wasteful modes of production – is something that individual Christians will have to face in the coming decades. While individual efforts are crucial most commentators realize that the transition to a more harmonious way of living will not be achieved without a major re-orientation of the economic and political systems in society. This will inevitably cause pain as some people lose out. They may experience hardship and suffering in the short term, even if in the long run the changes will mean an improvement in the quality of life for everyone.

As tensions arise conflicts, violence and perhaps even war may occur. Many people feel that friction about dwindling water rights may well spark the next war in the Middle East, North Africa or the Indian sub-continent. In the early 1990s a team of 30 researchers, working under the auspices of the University of Toronto and the American Academy of Arts and Sciences, addressed the issue of environmental change and acute conflict. They looked at a number of societies where resource shortages were occurring and insisted that these were contributing to violent conflicts in many parts of the world. They pointed out that land scarcity in Bangladesh had forced almost 15 million people to migrate to India. This in turn had led to fierce ethnic clashes.[9]

This potential for conflict inherent in the effort to achieve a just and ecologically sustainable way of living represents a particular challenge for the Church. It cannot be content with merely proposing and advocating new perspectives. Instead it must be willing to accompany the process of change, creating through its educational efforts and pastoral care the conditions which will help reduce the risk of disruption and disintegration.

A good example of what I am proposing is an American series of workshops entitled 'Jobs and the Environment'.[10] The workshops explore in a participatory way many of the issues involved in the tension between wishing to protect the environment and worrying about unemployment. Communities in many parts of the world are often faced with this kind of dilemma. Their choice seems to be between jobs or poison.

The initial activity looks at public attitudes towards jobs and the environment and whether the participants think that environmental quality is improving or not. Dialogue and sharing are central to the process. To facilitate this a range of relevant data is included to help the participants debate the issue in an effective way. For example, polls are quoted that show that most US citizens are concerned about the environment and think that environmental quality is declining. Nevertheless, when jobs are at stake their environmental concern diminishes.

The process then looks at the question of job security. It provides data on recent trends in the labour market which indicate that unemployment is rising and wages are falling, especially among working-class, manufacturing workers. These jobs are being re-placed by low-paid ones in the retail trade and other service areas. It acknowledges that many of the best-paying jobs are available in toxic-related industries, though even here companies are shedding workers. (One interesting statistic provided by the US Department of Labor is that unemployment is higher in States with extensive toxic-related industries.[11])

The third activity is designed to help the participants become more aware of environmental issues, especially the cost of environmental damage and clean-up. This activity is aimed at widening the horizons of the participants so that they can see the whole picture. It touches on environmental issues like global warming, ozone depletion, polluted groundwater and the rise in the number of people suffering and dying from cancer.

The next section concentrates more on providing information about the consequences of working in a chemical plant and ways in which chemicals are absorbed into the body. It lists some of the substances which are known to cause cancer in humans like asbestos and benzene. It also looks at the harm which can be done by chemicals to the human reproductive system. It concludes that a vast number of carcinogens are already in use and most are not properly regulated.

The fifth activity focuses on the proportion of the US economy which is involved in toxic-related activity. Huge segments of the economy – agriculture, transportation, electronics, petroleum, tobacco and a host of others – are toxic producers or consumers. While jobs in these areas are declining, the profits of the relevant corporations are rising. Toxic-related production accounts for an enormous amount of US wages, taxes and profits. Reducing this sector will have a huge impact on the economy and the lives of millions of people in the US and worldwide.

The next logical step in the process is to look at the subject of costs. Questions are asked about whether dangerous industries are really worth the trouble. Do the losses outweigh the gains? This session attempts to assess the cost of toxic industries in terms of human illness, deaths, the cost to taxpayers of regulatory agencies, compensation for accidents, and clean-up expenses. Included in the calculations are medical estimates for treating those who develop cancer and for compensating relatives of those who die from environmentally induced diseases. The estimate which the US Environmental Protection Agency (EPA) gives for a human life runs between $400,000 and $7 million. Putting a figure on the value of human life can be expected to give rise to a lively discussion. The overall conclusion is that the costs of toxic production are extremely high and liable to increase.

The seventh activity returns to the original question regarding the conflict between jobs and the environment. In the light of the previous discussion and data the participants can now look at the issue from a wider perspective. This includes recognizing some positive gains, for example that job opportunities exist in the area of pollution prevention and control. Some of the factual information in this section includes information on the size and power of large corporations: the top 500 corporations own 76 per cent of all US industrial assets. It argues that rising global corporate control of the economy causes both damage to the environment and job losses.

In their book *America: Who Really Pays Taxes?* Donal L. Barlett and James B. Steele discuss the case of Buster Brown Shoes. 'It managed, by means of some cunning detours through the Caymans, to reduce its 1987 tax rate to 1.7 per cent of sales. Meanwhile, the company was laying off hundreds of employees, who for their part had no choice but to pay taxes on the unemployment benefits.'[12] The authors also point out that in the 1950s, when corporate taxes were high, unemployment was low and the middle class was doing quite well. All that unfortunately has changed.

The final activity explores some possible solutions. These range across the spectrum of issues raised in this book: the need to control large corporations; fair trade versus free trade; pollution control technologies; recycling and clean technologies; the need for strong unions; and a knowledgeable and vigilant public.

The Church, which has access to Catholic universities and research facilities, should be well able to design similar accompanying programmes. In *Peace with God the Creator, Peace with All Creation* Pope John Paul II recognizes that 'an education in ecological responsibility is urgent. Churches and religious bodies, non-governmental and governmental organizations, indeed all members of society have a precise role to play in such education.'

Until now, Catholic schools have not been very different from their secular counterparts in terms of helping students to understand either the cry of the poor or the cry of the earth. They have followed the traditional educational pattern and trained economists, accountants, engineers, architects, doctors, lawyers, politicians, scientists, managers, teachers, and religious leaders who continue to be linchpins of the industrial age. Many of these graduates assume that it is legitimate to continue to exploit the earth without any thought of the consequences or the implications for the future. Seldom have they been challenged within the educational system to reflect on what is happening to the planet at large and, especially, the deterioration which is taking place in their own localities.

Catholic schools should set about developing programmes that help their students to have a comprehensive vision of the earth community. On the intellectual front this would involve introducing students to the story of the universe, covering such areas as the initial flaring forth, the shaping of the galaxies, the emergence of the solar system and planet Earth, the evolution of life on earth, and the dynamics of the local ecosystems.

Within this wider framework the students might be introduced to the development of human culture and especially the achievements and contributions of the classical civilizations and the religions. Since so much of the modern world is shaped by science and technology, courses might be designed to help students understand the enormous achievements involved here, but also the darker, more destructive side of the scientific/technological venture.

All of the above should be geared to facilitating the emergence of a new, less exploitative, sustainable relationship between humans and the rest of creation. On the practical side this will involve disseminating information about what different individuals and communities are doing to create a more just and sustainable society. Practical skills of self-reliance, basic crafts, appropriate technology and the rudiments of gardening and organic farming should also be included.

Those involved in education must encourage and nurture every glimmer of creativity in the arts, music, poetry, religion and science so that students are introduced to this wonderful world in a way that will allure and enchant them. Without this enchantment young people will find it difficult to disengage themselves from the present addictive and destructive patterns of living and evolve new personal and community lifestyles which are more in keeping with the contemporary challenge.

Some worthwhile material has already emerged. In Ireland, for example, the Columban Fathers and Sisters have produced sensitive environmental and development materials like *Windows on the World* and the *Gateway* series. In 1994 Trocaire, the Catholic Development Agency in Ireland, published *Team Planet*. This is a series of primary school texts which have been designed for use in both the Republic of Ireland and Northern Ireland. All of these texts assume that learning is a community venture which is promoted most effectively through dialogue and shared experience, and leads to social transformation and environmental sensitivity.

TRANSFORMING THE CHURCH

Pursuing this educational path would mean a conversion within the Church itself. It is difficult for an institution to promote dialogue, flexibility and openness among others if these are singularly lacking in its own life. It can make the institution appear irrelevant and hypocritical. Many of the same criticisms made about the World Bank and IMF are often directed against the Catholic Church. The leadership of the Catholic Church often acts in a top-down, secretive way. The process of choosing bishops is shrouded in secrecy, with little or no attempt to involve priests, religious or laity. Mechanisms of accountability are either non-existent or ineffective. Formulations of Catholic ethics, especially in the area of sexuality, are seen by many not to reflect the life experience of the vast majority of lay people. In churches in which they are excluded from Holy Orders women have a very muted voice in Church decisions.

NOTES

1 Robert Murray, *The Cosmic Covenant*, a Heythrop Monograph (London: Sheed and Ward, 1992), p. xx.
2 Ibid., p. 93: 'But the religion of the "cosmic covenant" and its maintenance was centred in the temple cult under the supervision of the sacral king. The cult has presuppositions and modes of action which are paralleled in many human cultures, and which must be called magical; but it was supremely concerned with *sedeq*, "rightness" in its whole range of meaning, cosmic, social and ethical, and with the establishment of *shalom*, which had and retains a similar range.'
3 Thomas Berry, 'The bush', private circulation (1994).
4 Bernard J. Cooke, *The Distancing of God* (Minneapolis: Fortress Press, 1990).
5 Sean McDonagh, *To Care for the Earth* (London: Geoffrey Chapman/Santa Fe, Bear & Co., 1986), pp. 161–8.
   A number of books containing creation and life-cycle liturgies have been published in recent years, including Rosemary Radford Ruether, *Women/ Church* (San Francisco: Harper & Row, 1985) and the St Hilda Community, *Women Included* (London: SPCK, 1991).
6 Beatrice Bruteau, 'Eucharistic ecology and ecological spirituality', *Cross Currents* (Winter 1990), p. 501.
7 Ibid., p. 502.
8 Barbara Wood, 'Simple lifestyle reexamined', *CAFOD Newsletter* (Autumn 1990), pp. 8–9.
9 Paul Hawken, *The Ecology of Commerce* (New York: HarperCollins, 1993), p. 24.
10 *Jobs and the Environment* (New York: Public Health Institute and the Labor Institute, 1994).
11 Data from the US Department of Labor, Bureau of Labor Statistics, *Employment and Earnings* (January 1993).
12 Quoted in Barbara Ehrenreich, 'Helping America's rich stay that way', *Time* (18 April 1994), p. 76.

Conclusion

I BEGAN THIS BOOK with a parable about a group of revellers who were enjoying a party without giving a thought to the social and environmental consequences of their carousing. I am sure that this behaviour appeared selfish, a bit simplistic and very stupid. Yet I am suggesting that there is a similarity between the attitude of those revellers and the people who are benefiting from our modern, throw-away and exploitative global economic system. In the latter, a small minority benefit while hundreds of millions suffer and the future fruitfulness of the earth itself is endangered.

During the past decade more and more people have become aware of global as well as local environmental and development problems. Reports about global warming, ozone depletion, malnutrition and famine figure regularly in the local, national and international media. Often the analysis is superficial and there is little attempt to present a comprehensive picture of what is happening to the poor and the earth. Nevertheless many significant initiatives have been taken at local and international level to respond to poverty and environmental degradation.

In the 1980s the United Nations World Commission on Environment and Development under the leadership of Gro Brundtland, the Prime Minister of Norway, studied these challenges and made several proposals in the area of food security, population programmes, biodiversity, energy policies and the need for closer North/South co-operation. The analysis and recommendations are published in the book appropriately named *Our Common Future*.

In a follow-up to this, the United Nations Conference on Environment and Development (UNCED) met in Rio de Janeiro in June 1992. Delegates from almost every country and an unprecedented number of heads of state attended that meeting. Once again the problems of deforestation, population growth, poverty and global pollution were discussed and a number of initiatives were proposed to address them.

Both these events indicate that the issues of environment and development are gradually making their way on to the political agenda at the national and global level. The difficulty is that politicians, economists and the public in the North think that solutions can be found in a more or less business-as-usual approach which promotes rapid economic growth while attempting to alleviate the ugly face of development through a variety of technological fixes.

In *Passion for the Earth* I have disagreed with that analysis. In the chapters on GATT and the multilateral lending agencies I argued that the present policies exacerbate the division between the rich and the poor and destroy vital ecosystems.

In Chapter 4 I insisted, with a growing number of ecologists and economists, that the Earth's resources are limited. The most important task facing contemporary human society is to devise a way of living that respects limits and yet ensures that people's basic needs are met. Sustainability must become more than a catchword: it should be the central organizing principle for every human activity – from food production to energy use, security and waste management.

Living in a sustainable way requires major changes at both the personal and the institutional levels. At the personal level people, especially those in the affluent North and the élite in the South, will have to live more simply. But changes on the part of individuals will be of little help and will probably not perdure unless they are supported by changes at the institutional level. These changes need to take place in education, media, industry, commerce, in short, in all aspects of human activity.

Religions do not escape this call for change. Building on what I have already written in *To Care for the Earth* and *The Greening of the Church*, I have explored what contribution religion, in particular the Catholic Church, can make to the contemporary task of living in a sustainable way. I have suggested that the prophetic ministry should focus on this task by critiquing the present inequitable system and by kindling the imagination of Christians individually and as a community to picturing new, sustainable ways of living. Religious groups must also develop theologies, catechesis, liturgies and pastoral initiatives that take creation and the present situation seriously.

In *The Greening of the Church* I stressed the role of prayer in developing an environmental consciousness. In the section on the Psalms I wrote that 'the motif of praising God as creator is almost as common as praising God as saviour of his people'.[1] I will not repeat what I have said there and also in *To Care for the Earth* on the link between environment and prayer. But I will end this book on Justice, Peace and the Integrity of Creation with a prayer. This prayer has not come from a modern New Age community. It is almost as old as the Church, from the pen of St Basil, a key figure in the patristic era.

O God, enlarge within us a sense of fellowship with all living things, our brothers and sisters the animals, to whom thou gavest the earth as their home in common with us.

We remember with shame that in the past we have exercised the high dominion of man with ruthless cruelty, so that the voice of the earth, which should have gone up to you in song, has been a groan of travail.

May we realize that they live not for us alone but for themselves and for thee, and that they love the sweetness of life.

NOTE
1 Sean McDonagh, *The Greening of the Church* (London: Geoffrey Chapman/ Maryknoll, NY: Orbis Books, 1990), p. 147.

Fr Sean McDonagh is an Irish Columban missionary who has worked in the Philippines for 20 years, mainly among the T'boli people. At present he is the central co-ordinator for Justice, Peace and the Integrity of Creation for the Columban missionaries. He is also chairperson of Greenpeace, Ireland.

SSND JPIC